Prince Zaleski

M. P. Shiel

Alpha Editions

This edition published in 2024

ISBN 9789362098207

Design and Setting By
Alpha Editions
www.alphaedis.com
Email - info@alphaedis.com

As per information held with us this book is in Public Domain.
This book is a reproduction of an important historical work.
Alpha Editions uses the best technology to reproduce historical work
in the same manner it was first published to preserve its original nature.
Any marks or number seen are left intentionally to preserve.

Contents

THE RACE OF ORVEN	- 1 -
THE STONE OF THE EDMUNDSBURY MONKS	- 25 -
THE S.S.	- 42 -

THE RACE OF ORVEN

Never without grief and pain could I remember the fate of Prince Zaleski—victim of a too importunate, too unfortunate Love, which the fulgor of the throne itself could not abash; exile perforce from his native land, and voluntary exile from the rest of men! Having renounced the world, over which, lurid and inscrutable as a falling star, he had passed, the world quickly ceased to wonder at him; and even I, to whom, more than to another, the workings of that just and passionate mind had been revealed, half forgot him in the rush of things.

But during the time that what was called the 'Pharanx labyrinth' was exercising many of the heaviest brains in the land, my thought turned repeatedly to him; and even when the affair had passed from the general attention, a bright day in Spring, combined perhaps with a latent mistrust of the *dénoûment* of that dark plot, drew me to his place of hermitage.

I reached the gloomy abode of my friend as the sun set. It was a vast palace of the older world standing lonely in the midst of woodland, and approached by a sombre avenue of poplars and cypresses, through which the sunlight hardly pierced. Up this I passed, and seeking out the deserted stables (which I found all too dilapidated to afford shelter) finally put up my *calèche* in the ruined sacristy of an old Dominican chapel, and turned my mare loose to browse for the night on a paddock behind the domain.

As I pushed back the open front door and entered the mansion, I could not but wonder at the saturnine fancy that had led this wayward man to select a brooding-place so desolate for the passage of his days. I regarded it as a vast tomb of Mausolus in which lay deep sepulchred how much genius, culture, brilliancy, power! The hall was constructed in the manner of a Roman *atrium*, and from the oblong pool of turgid water in the centre a troop of fat and otiose rats fled weakly squealing at my approach. I mounted by broken marble steps to the corridors running round the open space, and thence pursued my way through a mazeland of apartments—suite upon suite—along many a length of passage, up and down many stairs. Dust-clouds rose from the uncarpeted floors and choked me; incontinent Echo coughed answering *ricochets* to my footsteps in the gathering darkness, and added emphasis to the funereal gloom of the dwelling. Nowhere was there a vestige of furniture—nowhere a trace of human life.

After a long interval I came, in a remote tower of the building and near its utmost summit, to a richly-carpeted passage, from the ceiling of which three mosaic lamps shed dim violet, scarlet and pale-rose lights around. At the end I perceived two figures standing as if in silent guard on each side of a door tapestried with the python's skin. One was a post-replica in Parian marble of the nude Aphrodite of Cnidus; in the other I recognised the gigantic form of the negro Ham, the prince's only attendant, whose fierce, and glistening, and ebon visage broadened into a grin of intelligence as I came nearer. Nodding to him, I pushed without ceremony into Zaleski's apartment.

The room was not a large one, but lofty. Even in the semi-darkness of the very faint greenish lustre radiated from an open censerlike *lampas* of fretted gold in the centre of the domed encausted roof, a certain incongruity of barbaric gorgeousness in the furnishing filled me with amazement. The air was heavy with the scented odour of this light, and the fumes of the narcotic *cannabis sativa*—the base of the *bhang* of the Mohammedans—in which I knew it to be the habit of my friend to assuage himself. The hangings were of wine-coloured velvet, heavy, gold-fringed and embroidered at Nurshedabad. All the world knew Prince Zaleski to be a consummate *cognoscente*—a profound amateur—as well as a savant and a thinker; but I was, nevertheless, astounded at the mere multitudinousness of the curios he had contrived to crowd into the space around him. Side by side rested a palaeolithic implement, a Chinese 'wise man,' a Gnostic gem, an amphora of Graeco-Etruscan work. The general effect was a *bizarrerie* of half-weird sheen and gloom. Flemish sepulchral brasses companied strangely with runic tablets, miniature paintings, a winged bull, Tamil scriptures on lacquered leaves of the talipot, mediaeval reliquaries richly gemmed, Brahmin gods. One whole side of the room was occupied by an organ whose thunder in that circumscribed place must have set all these relics of dead epochs clashing and jingling in fantastic dances. As I entered, the vaporous atmosphere was palpitating to the low, liquid tinkling of an invisible musical box. The prince reclined on a couch from which a draping of cloth-of-silver rolled torrent over the floor. Beside him, stretched in its open sarcophagus which rested on three brazen trestles, lay the mummy of an ancient Memphian, from the upper part of which the brown cerements had rotted or been rent, leaving the hideousness of the naked, grinning countenance exposed to view.

Discarding his gemmed chibouque and an old vellum reprint of Anacreon, Zaleski rose hastily and greeted me with warmth, muttering at the same time some commonplace about his 'pleasure' and the 'unexpectedness' of my visit. He then gave orders to Ham to prepare me a bed in one of the adjoining chambers. We passed the greater part of the night in a delightful stream of that somnolent and half-mystic talk which Prince Zaleski alone could initiate and sustain, during which he repeatedly pressed on me a concoction of Indian hemp resembling *hashish*, prepared by his own hands, and quite innocuous. It was after a simple breakfast the next morning that I entered on the subject which was partly the occasion of my visit. He lay back on his couch, volumed in a Turkish *beneesh*, and listened to me, a little wearily perhaps at first, with woven fingers, and the pale inverted eyes of old anchorites and astrologers, the moony greenish light falling on his always wan features.

'You knew Lord Pharanx?' I asked.

'I have met him in "the world." His son Lord Randolph, too, I saw once at Court at Peterhof, and once again at the Winter Palace of the Tsar. I noticed in their great stature, shaggy heads of hair, ears of a very peculiar conformation, and a certain aggressiveness of demeanour—a strong likeness between father and son.'

I had brought with me a bundle of old newspapers, and comparing these as I went on, I proceeded to lay the incidents before him.

'The father,' I said, 'held, as you know, high office in a late Administration, and was one of our big luminaries in politics; he has also been President of the Council of several learned societies, and author of a book on Modern Ethics. His son was rapidly rising to eminence in the *corps diplomatique*, and lately (though, strictly speaking, *unebenbürtig*) contracted an affiance with the Prinzessin Charlotte Mariana Natalia of Morgen-üppigen, a lady with a strain of indubitable Hohenzollern blood in her royal veins. The Orven family is a very old and distinguished one, though—especially in modern days—far from wealthy. However, some little time after Randolph had become engaged to this royal lady, the father insured his life for immense sums in various offices both in England and America, and the reproach of poverty is now swept from the race. Six months ago, almost simultaneously, both father and son resigned their various positions *en bloc*. But all this, of course, I am telling you on the assumption that you have not already read it in the papers.'

'A modern newspaper,' he said, 'being what it mostly is, is the one thing insupportable to me at present. Believe me, I never see one.'

'Well, then, Lord Pharanx, as I said, threw up his posts in the fulness of his vigour, and retired to one of his country seats. A good many years ago, he and Randolph had a terrible row over some trifle, and, with the implacability that distinguishes their race, had not since exchanged a word. But some little time after the retirement of the father, a message was despatched by him to the son, who was then in India. Considered as the first step in the *rapprochement* of this proud and selfish pair of beings, it was an altogether remarkable message, and was subsequently deposed to in evidence by a telegraph official; it ran:

"'*Return. The beginning of the end is come.*" Whereupon Randolph did return, and in three months from the date of his landing in England, Lord Pharanx was dead.'

'*Murdered?*'

A certain something in the tone in which this word was uttered by Zaleski puzzled me. It left me uncertain whether he had addressed to me an exclamation of conviction, or a simple question. I must have looked this feeling, for he said at once:

'I could easily, from your manner, surmise as much, you know. Perhaps I might even have foretold it, years ago.'

'Foretold—what? Not the murder of Lord Pharanx?'

'Something of that kind,' he answered with a smile; 'but proceed—tell me all the facts you know.'

Word-mysteries of this sort fell frequent from the lips of the prince. I continued the narrative.

'The two, then, met, and were reconciled. But it was a reconciliation without cordiality, without affection—a shaking of hands across a barrier of brass; and even this hand-shaking was a strictly metaphorical one, for they do not seem ever to have got beyond the interchange of a frigid bow. The opportunities, however, for observation were few. Soon after Randolph's arrival at Orven Hall, his father entered on a life of the most absolute seclusion. The mansion is an old three-storied one, the top floor consisting for the most part of sleeping-rooms, the first of a library, drawing-room, and so on, and the ground-floor, in addition to the dining and other ordinary rooms, of another small library, looking out (at the side of the house) on a low balcony, which, in turn, looks on a lawn dotted with flower-beds. It was this smaller library on the ground-floor that was now divested of its books, and converted into a bedroom for the earl. Hither he migrated, and here he lived, scarcely ever leaving it. Randolph, on his part, moved to a room on the first floor immediately above this. Some of the retainers of the family were dismissed, and on the remaining few fell a hush of expectancy, a sense of wonder, as to what these things boded. A great enforced quiet pervaded the building, the least undue noise in any part being sure to be followed by the angry voice of the master demanding the cause. Once, as the servants were supping in the kitchen on the side of the house most remote from that which he occupied, Lord Pharanx, slippered and in dressing-gown, appeared at the doorway, purple with rage, threatening to pack the whole company of them out of doors if they did not moderate the clatter of their knives and forks. He had always been regarded with fear in his own household, and the very sound of his voice now became a terror. His food was taken to him in the room he had made his habitation, and it was remarked that, though simple before in his gustatory tastes, he now—possibly owing to the sedentary life he led—became fastidious, insisting on *recherché* bits. I mention all these details to you—as I shall mention others—not because they have the least connection with the tragedy as it subsequently occurred, but merely because I know them, and you have requested me to state all I know.'

'Yes,' he answered, with a suspicion of *ennui*, 'you are right. I may as well hear the whole—if I must hear a part.'

'Meanwhile, Randolph appears to have visited the earl at least once a day. In such retirement did he, too, live that many of his friends still supposed him to be in India. There was only one respect in which he broke through this privacy. You know, of course, that the Orvens are, and, I believe, always have been, noted as the most obstinate, the most crabbed of Conservatives in politics. Even among the past-enamoured families of England, they stand out conspicuously in this respect. Is it credible to you, then, that Randolph should offer himself to the Radical Association of the Borough of Orven as a candidate for the next election in opposition to the sitting member? It is on record, too, that he spoke at three public meetings—reported in local papers—at which he avowed his political conversion; afterwards laid the foundation-stone of a new Baptist chapel; presided at a Methodist tea-meeting; and taking an abnormal interest in the debased condition of the labourers in the villages round, fitted up as a class-room an apartment on the top floor at Orven Hall, and gathered round him on two evenings in every week a class of yokels, whom he proceeded to cram with demonstrations in elementary mechanics.'

'Mechanics!' cried Zaleski, starting upright for a moment, 'mechanics to agricultural labourers! Why not elementary chemistry? Why not elementary botany? *Why* mechanics?'

This was the first evidence of interest he had shown in the story. I was pleased, but answered:

'The point is unimportant; and there really is no accounting for the vagaries of such a man. He wished, I imagine, to give some idea to the young illiterates of the simple laws of motion and force. But now I come to a new character in the drama—the chief character of all. One day a woman presented herself at Orven Hall and demanded to see its owner. She spoke English with a strong French accent. Though approaching middle life she was still beautiful, having wild black eyes, and creamy pale face. Her dress was tawdry, cheap, and loud, showing signs of wear; her hair was unkempt; her manners were not the manners of a lady. A certain vehemence, exasperation, unrepose distinguished all she said and did. The footman refused her admission; Lord Pharanx, he said, was invisible. She persisted violently, pushed past him, and had to be forcibly ejected; during all which the voice of the master was heard roaring from the passage red-eyed remonstrance at the unusual noise. She went away gesticulating wildly, and vowing vengeance on Lord Pharanx and all the world. It was afterwards found that she had taken up her abode in one of the neighbouring hamlets, called Lee.

'This person, who gave the name of Maude Cibras, subsequently called at the Hall three times in succession, and was each time refused admittance. It was now, however, thought advisable to inform Randolph of her visits. He said she might be permitted to see him, if she returned. This she did on the next day, and had a long interview in private with him. Her voice was heard raised as if in angry protest by one Hester Dyett, a servant of the house, while Randolph in low tones seemed to try to soothe her. The conversation was in French, and no word could be made out. She passed out at length, tossing her head jauntily, and smiling a vulgar triumph at the footman who had before opposed her ingress. She was never known to seek admission to the house again.

'But her connection with its inmates did not cease. The same Hester asserts that one night, coming home late through the park, she saw two persons conversing on a bench beneath the trees, crept behind some bushes, and discovered that they were the strange woman and Randolph. The same servant bears evidence to tracking them to other meeting-places, and to finding in the letter-bag letters addressed to Maude Cibras in Randolph's hand-writing. One of these was actually unearthed later on. Indeed, so engrossing did the intercourse become, that it seems even to have interfered with the outburst of radical zeal in the new political convert. The *rendezvous*—always held under cover of darkness, but naked and open to the eye of the watchful Hester—sometimes clashed with the science lectures, when these latter would be put off, so that they became gradually fewer, and then almost ceased.'

'Your narrative becomes unexpectedly interesting,' said Zaleski; 'but this unearthed letter of Randolph's—what was in it?'

I read as follows:

"'Dear Mdlle. Cibras,—I am exerting my utmost influence for you with my father. But he shows no signs of coming round as yet. If I could only induce him to see you! But he is, as you know, a person of unrelenting will, and meanwhile you must confide in my loyal efforts on your behalf. At the same time, I admit that the situation is a precarious one: you are, I am sure, well provided for in the present will of Lord Pharanx, but he is on the point—within, say, three or four days—of making another; and exasperated as he is at your appearance in England, I know there is no chance of your receiving a *centime* under the new will. Before then, however, we must hope that something favourable to you may happen; and in the meantime, let me implore you not to let your only too just resentment pass beyond the bounds of reason.

"Sincerely yours,

"RANDOLPH.'"

'I like the letter!' cried Zaleski. 'You notice the tone of manly candour. But the *facts*—were they true? *Did* the earl make a new will in the time specified?'

'No,—but that may have been because his death intervened.'

'And in the old will, *was* Mdlle. Cibras provided for?'

'Yes,—that at least was correct.'

A shadow of pain passed over his face.

'And now,' I went on, 'I come to the closing scene, in which one of England's foremost men perished by the act of an obscure assassin. The letter I have read was written to Maude Cibras on the 5th of January. The next thing that happens is on the 6th, when Lord Pharanx left his room for another during the whole day, and a skilled mechanic was introduced into it for the purpose of effecting some alterations. Asked by Hester Dyett, as he was leaving the house, what was the nature of his operations, the man replied that he had been applying a patent arrangement to the window looking out on the balcony, for the better protection of the room against burglars, several robberies having recently been committed in the neighbourhood. The sudden death of this man, however, before the occurrence of the tragedy, prevented his evidence being heard. On the next day—the 7th—Hester, entering the room with Lord Pharanx's dinner, fancies, though she cannot tell why (inasmuch as his back is towards her, he sitting in an arm-chair by the fire), that Lord Pharanx has been "drinking heavily."

'On the 8th a singular thing befell. The earl was at last induced to see Maude Cibras, and during the morning of that day, with his own hand, wrote a note informing her of his decision, Randolph handing the note to a messenger. That note also has been made public. It reads as follows:

"'Maude Cibras.—You may come here to-night after dark. Walk to the south side of the house, come up the steps to the balcony, and pass in through the open window to my room. Remember, however, that you have nothing to expect from me, and that from to-night I blot you eternally from my mind: but I will hear your story, which I know beforehand to be false. Destroy this note. PHARANX."'

As I progressed with my tale, I came to notice that over the countenance of Prince Zaleski there grew little by little a singular fixed aspect. His small, keen features distorted themselves into an expression of what I can only describe as an abnormal *inquisitiveness* —an inquisitiveness most impatient, arrogant, in its intensity. His pupils, contracted each to a dot, became the central *puncta* of two rings of fiery light; his little sharp teeth seemed to gnash. Once before I had seen him look thus greedily, when, grasping a Troglodyte tablet covered with half-effaced hieroglyphics—his fingers livid with the fixity of his grip—he bent on it that strenuous inquisition, that ardent questioning gaze, till, by a species of mesmeric dominancy, he seemed to wrench from it the arcanum it hid from other eyes; then he lay back, pale and faint from the too arduous victory.

When I had read Lord Pharanx's letter, he took the paper eagerly from my hand, and ran his eyes over the passage.

'Tell me—the end,' he said.

'Maude Cibras,' I went on, 'thus invited to a meeting with the earl, failed to make her appearance at the appointed time. It happened that she had left her lodgings in the village early that very morning, and, for some purpose or other, had travelled to the town of Bath. Randolph, too, went away the same day in the opposite direction to Plymouth. He returned on the following morning, the 9th; soon after walked over to Lee; and entered into conversation with the keeper of the inn where Cibras lodged; asked if she was at home, and on being told that she had gone away, asked further if she had taken her luggage with her; was informed that she had, and had also announced her intention of at once leaving England. He then walked away in the direction of the Hall. On this day Hester Dyett noticed that there were many articles of value scattered about the earl's room, notably a tiara of old Brazilian brilliants, sometimes worn by the late Lady Pharanx. Randolph—who was present at the time—further drew her attention to these by telling her that Lord Pharanx had chosen to bring together in his apartment many of the family jewels; and she was instructed to tell the other servants of this fact, in case they should notice any suspicious-looking loafers about the estate.

'On the 10th, both father and son remained in their rooms all day, except when the latter came down to meals; at which times he would lock his door behind him, and with his own hands take in the earl's food, giving as his reason that his father was writing a very important document, and did not wish to be disturbed by the presence of a servant. During the forenoon, Hester Dyett, hearing loud noises in Randolph's room, as if furniture was being removed from place to place, found some pretext for knocking at his door, when he ordered her on no account to interrupt him again, as he was busy packing his clothes in view of a journey to London on the next day. The subsequent conduct of the woman shows that her curiosity must have been excited to the utmost by the undoubtedly strange spectacle of Randolph packing his own clothes. During the afternoon a lad from the village was instructed to collect his companions for a science lecture the same evening at eight o'clock. And so the eventful day wore on.

'We arrive now at this hour of eight P.M. on this 10th day of January. The night is dark and windy; some snow has been falling, but has now ceased. In an upper room is Randolph engaged in expounding the elements of dynamics; in the room under that is Hester Dyett—for Hester has somehow obtained a key that opens the door of Randolph's room, and takes advantage of his absence upstairs to explore it. Under her is Lord Pharanx, certainly in bed, probably asleep. Hester, trembling all over in a fever of fear and excitement, holds a lighted taper in one hand, which she religiously shades with the other; for the storm is gusty, and the gusts, tearing through the crevices of the rattling old casements, toss great flickering shadows on the hangings, which frighten her to death. She has just time to see that the whole room is in the wildest confusion, when suddenly a rougher puff blows out the flame, and she is left in what to her, standing as she was on that forbidden ground, must have been a horror of darkness. At the same moment, clear and sharp from right beneath her, a pistol-shot rings out on her ear. For an instant she stands in stone, incapable of motion. Then on her dazed senses there supervenes—so she swore—the consciousness that some object is moving in the room— moving apparently of its own accord—moving in direct opposition to all the laws of nature as she knows them. She imagines that she perceives a phantasm—a strange something—globular-white—looking, as she says, "like a good-sized ball of cotton"—rise directly from the floor before her, ascending slowly upward, as if driven aloft by some invisible force. A sharp shock of the sense of the supernatural deprives her of ordered reason. Throwing forward her arms, and uttering a shrill scream, she rushes towards the door. But she never reaches it: midway she falls prostrate over some object, and knows no more; and when, an hour later, she is borne out of the room in the arms of Randolph himself, the blood is dripping from a fracture of her right tibia.

'Meantime, in the upper chamber the pistol-shot and the scream of the woman have been heard. All eyes turn to Randolph. He stands in the shadow of the mechanical contrivance on which he has been illustrating his points; leans for support on it. He essays to speak, the muscles of his face work, but no sound comes. Only after a time is he able to gasp: "Did you hear something—from below?" They answer "yes" in chorus; then one of the lads takes a lighted candle, and together they troop out, Randolph behind them. A terrified servant rushes up with the news that something dreadful has happened in the house. They proceed for some distance, but there is an open window on the stairs, and the light is blown out. They have to wait some minutes till another is obtained, and then the procession moves forward once more. Arrived at Lord Pharanx's door, and finding it locked, a lantern is procured, and Randolph leads them through the house and out on the lawn. But having nearly reached the balcony, a lad observes a track of small woman's-feet in the snow; a halt is called, and then Randolph points out another track of feet, half obliterated by the snow, extending from a coppice close by up to the balcony, and forming an angle with the first track. These latter are great big feet, made by ponderous labourers' boots. He holds the lantern over the flower-beds, and shows how they have been trampled down. Some one finds a common scarf, such as workmen wear; and a ring and a locket, dropped by the burglars in their flight, are also found by Randolph half buried in the snow. And now the foremost reach the window. Randolph, from behind, calls to them to enter. They cry back that they cannot, the window being closed. At this reply he seems to be overcome by surprise, by terror. Some one hears him murmur the words, "My God, what can have happened now?" His horror is increased when one of the lads bears to him a revolting trophy, which has been found just outside the window; it is the front phalanges of three fingers of a human hand. Again he utters the agonised moan, "My God!" and then, mastering his agitation, makes for the window; he finds that the catch of the sash has been roughly wrenched off, and that the sash can be opened by merely pushing it up: does so, and enters. The room is in darkness: on the floor under the window is found the insensible body of the woman Cibras. She is alive, but has fainted. Her right fingers are closed round the handle of a large bowie-knife, which is covered with blood; parts of the left are missing. All the jewelry has been stolen from the room. Lord Pharanx lies on the bed, stabbed through the bedclothes to the heart. Later on a bullet is also found imbedded in his brain. I should explain that a trenchant edge, running along the bottom of the sash, was the obvious means by which the fingers of Cibras had been cut off. This had been placed there a few days before by the workman I spoke of. Several secret springs had been placed on the inner side of the lower horizontal piece of the window-frame, by pressing any one of which the sash was lowered; so that no one, ignorant of the secret, could pass out from within, without resting the hand on one of these springs, and so bringing down the armed sash suddenly on the underlying hand.

'There was, of course, a trial. The poor culprit, in mortal terror of death, shrieked out a confession of the murder just as the jury had returned from their brief consultation, and before they had time to pronounce their verdict of "guilty." But she denied shooting Lord Pharanx, and she denied stealing the jewels; and indeed no pistol and no jewels were found on her, or anywhere in the room. So that many points remain mysterious. What part did the burglars play in the tragedy? Were they in collusion with Cibras? Had the strange behaviour of at least one of the inmates of Orven Hall no hidden significance? The wildest guesses were made throughout the country; theories propounded. But no theory explained *all* the points. The ferment, however, has now subsided. To-morrow morning Maude Cibras ends her life on the gallows.'

Thus I ended my narrative.

Without a word Zaleski rose from the couch, and walked to the organ. Assisted from behind by Ham, who foreknew his master's every whim, he proceeded to render with infinite feeling an air from the *Lakmé* of Delibes; long he sat, dreamily uttering the melody, his head sunken on his breast. When at last he rose, his great expanse of brow was clear, and a smile all but solemn in its serenity was on his lips. He walked up to an ivory *escritoire*, scribbled a few words on a sheet of paper, and handed it to the negro with the order to take my trap and drive with the message in all haste to the nearest telegraph office.

'That message,' he said, resuming his place on the couch, 'is a last word on the tragedy, and will, no doubt, produce some modification in the final stage of its history. And now, Shiel, let us sit together and confer on this matter. From the manner in which you have expressed yourself, it is evident that there are points which puzzle you—you do not get a clean *coup d'oeil* of the whole regiment of facts, and their causes, and their consequences, as they occurred. Let us see if out of that confusion we cannot produce a coherence, a symmetry. A great wrong is done, and on the society in which it is done is imposed the task of making it translucent, of seeing it in all its relations, and of punishing it. But what happens? The society fails to rise to the occasion; on the whole, it contrives to make the opacity more opaque, does not see the crime in any human sense; is unable to punish it. Now this, you will admit, whenever it occurs, is a woful failure: woful I mean, not very in itself, but very in its significance: and there must be a precise cause for it. That cause is the lack of something not merely, or specially, in the investigators of the wrong, but in the world at large—shall we not boldly call it the lack of culture? Do not, however, misunderstand me: by the term I mean not so much attainment in general, as *mood* in particular. Whether or when such mood may become universal may be to you a matter of doubt. As for me, I often think that when the era of civilisation begins—as assuredly it shall some day begin—when the races of the world cease to be credulous, ovine mobs and become critical, human nations, then will be the ushering in of the ten thousand years of a *clairvoyant* culture. But nowhere, and at no time during the very few hundreds of years that man has occupied the earth, has there been one single sign of its presence. In individuals, yes—in the Greek Plato, and I think in your English Milton and Bishop Berkeley—but in humanity, never; and hardly in any individual outside those two nations. The reason, I fancy, is not so much that man is a hopeless fool, as that Time, so far as he is concerned, has, as we know, only just begun: it being, of course, conceivable that the creation of a perfect society of men, as the first requisite to a *régime* of culture, must nick to itself a longer loop of time than the making of, say, a stratum of coal. A loquacious person—he is one of your cherished "novel"-writers, by the way, if that be indeed a Novel in which there is nowhere any pretence at novelty—once assured me that he could never reflect without swelling on the greatness of the age in which he lived, an age the mighty civilisation of which he likened to the Augustan and Periclean. A certain stony gaze of anthropological interest with which I regarded his frontal bone seemed to strike the poor man dumb, and he took a hurried departure. Could he have been ignorant that ours is, in general, greater than the Periclean for the very reason that the Divinity is neither the devil nor a bungler; that three thousand years of human consciousness is not nothing; that a whole is greater than its part, and a butterfly than a chrysalis? But it was the assumption that it was therefore in any way great in the abstract that occasioned my profound astonishment, and indeed contempt. Civilisation, if it means anything, can only mean the art by which men live musically together—to the lutings, as it were, of Panpipes, or say perhaps, to triumphant organ-bursts of martial, marching dithyrambs. Any formula defining it as "the art of lying back and getting elaborately tickled," should surely at this hour be *too* primitive—*too* Opic—to bring anything but a smile to the lips of grown white-skinned men; and the very fact that such a definition can still find undoubting acceptance in all quarters may be an indication that the true [Greek: *idéa*] which this condition of being must finally assume is far indeed—far, perhaps, by ages and aeons—from becoming part of the general conception. Nowhere since the beginning has the gross problem of living ever so much as approached solution, much less the delicate and intricate one of living *together: à propos* of which your body corporate not only still produces criminals (as the body-natural fleas), but its very elementary organism cannot so much as catch a really athletic one as yet. Meanwhile *you* and *I* are handicapped. The individual travaileth in pain. In the struggle for quality, powers, air, he spends his strength, and yet hardly escapes asphyxiation. He can no more wriggle himself free of the psychic gravitations that invest him than the earth can shake herself loose of the sun, or he of the omnipotences that rivet him to the universe. If by chance one shoots a downy hint of wings, an instant feeling of contrast puffs him with self-consciousness: a tragedy at once: the unconscious being "the alone complete." To attain to anything, he must needs screw the head up into the atmosphere of the future, while feet and hands drip dark ichors of despair from the crucifying cross of the crude present—*a horrid strain*! Far up a nightly instigation of stars he sees: but he may not strike them with the head. If earth were a boat, and mine, I know well toward what wild azimuths I would compel her helm: but gravity, gravity—chiefest curse of Eden's sin!—is hostile. When indeed (as is ordained), the old mother swings herself into a sublimer orbit, we on her back will follow: till then we make to ourselves Icarian "organa" in vain. I mean to say that it is the plane of station which is at fault: move that upward, you move all. But meantime is it not Goethe who assures us that "further reacheth no man, make he what stretching he will"? For Man, you perceive, is not many, but One. It is absurd to suppose that England can be free while Poland is enslaved; Paris is *far* from the beginnings of civilisation whilst Toobooloo and Chicago are barbaric. Probably no ill-fated, microcephalous son of Adam ever tumbled into a mistake quite so huge, so infantile, as did Dives, if he imagined himself rich while Lazarus sat pauper at the gate. Not many, I say, but one. Even Ham and I here in our retreat are not alone; we are embarrassed by the uninvited spirit of the present; the adamant root of the mountain on whose summit we stand is based ineradicably in the low world. Yet, thank Heaven, Goethe was not *quite* right—as, indeed, he proved in his proper person. I tell you, Shiel, I *know* whether Mary did or did not murder Darnley; I know—as clearly, as precisely, as a man can know—that Beatrice Cenci was not "guilty" as certain recently-discovered documents "prove" her, but that the Shelley version of the affair, though a guess, is the correct one. It *is* possible, by taking thought, to add one cubit—or say a hand, or a dactyl—to your stature; you may develop powers slightly—very slightly, but distinctly, both in kind and degree—in advance of those of the mass who live in or about the same cycle of time in which you live. But it is only when the powers to which I refer are shared by the mass—when what, for want of another term, I call the age of the Cultured Mood has at length arrived—

that their exercise will become easy and familiar to the individual; and who shall say what presciences, prisms, *séances*, what introspective craft, Genie apocalypses, shall not *then* become possible to the few who stand spiritually in the van of men.

'All this, you will understand, I say as some sort of excuse for myself, and for you, for any hesitation we may have shown in loosening the very little puzzle you have placed before me—one which we certainly must not regard as difficult of solution. Of course, looking at all the facts, the first consideration that must inevitably rivet the attention is that arising from the circumstance that Viscount Randolph has strong reasons to wish his father dead. They are avowed enemies; he is the *fiancé* of a princess whose husband he is probably too poor to become, though he will very likely be rich enough when his father dies; and so on. All that appears on the surface. On the other hand, we—you and I—know the man: he is a person of gentle blood, as moral, we suppose, as ordinary people, occupying a high station in the world. It is impossible to imagine that such a person would commit an assassination, or even countenance one, for any or all of the reasons that present themselves. In our hearts, with or without clear proof, we could hardly believe it of him. Earls' sons do not, in fact, go about murdering people. Unless, then, we can so reason as to discover other motives— strong, adequate, irresistible—and by "irresistible" I mean a motive which must be *far* stronger than even the love of life itself—we should, I think, in fairness dismiss him from our mind.

'And yet it must be admitted that his conduct is not free of blame. He contracts a sudden intimacy with the acknowledged culprit, whom he does not seem to have known before. He meets her by night, corresponds with her. Who and what is this woman? I think we could not be far wrong in guessing some very old flame of Lord Pharanx's of *Théâtre des Variétés* type, whom he has supported for years, and from whom, hearing some story to her discredit, he threatens to withdraw his supplies. However that be, Randolph writes to Cibras—a violent woman, a woman of lawless passions—assuring her that in four or five days she will be excluded from the will of his father; and in four or five days Cibras plunges a knife into his father's bosom. It is a perfectly natural sequence—though, of course, the *intention* to produce by his words the actual effect produced might have been absent; indeed, the letter of Lord Pharanx himself, had it been received, would have tended to produce that very effect; for it not only gives an excellent opportunity for converting into action those evil thoughts which Randolph (thoughtlessly or guiltily) has instilled, but it further tends to rouse her passions by cutting off from her all hopes of favour. If we presume, then, as is only natural, that there was no such intention on the part of the earl, we *may* make the same presumption in the case of the son.

Cibras, however, never receives the earl's letter: on the morning of the same day she goes away to Bath, with the double object, I suppose, of purchasing a weapon, and creating an impression that she has left the country. How then does she know the exact *locale* of Lord Pharanx's room? It is in an unusual part of the mansion, she is unacquainted with any of the servants, a stranger to the district. Can it be possible that Randolph *had told her*? And here again, even in that case, you must bear in mind that Lord Pharanx also told her in his note, and you must recognise the possibility of the absence of evil intention on the part of the son. Indeed, I may go further and show you that in all but every instance in which his actions are in themselves *outré*, suspicious, they are rendered, not less *outré*, but less suspicious, by the fact that Lord Pharanx himself knew of them, shared in them. There was the cruel barbing of that balcony window; about it the crudest thinker would argue thus to himself: "Randolph practically incites Maude Cibras to murder his father on the 5th, and on the 6th he has that window so altered in order that, should she act on his suggestion, she will be caught on attempting to leave the room, while he himself, the actual culprit being discovered *en flagrant délit*, will escape every shadow of suspicion." But, on the other hand, we know that the alteration was made with Lord Pharanx's consent, most likely on his initiative—for he leaves his favoured room during a whole day for that very purpose. So with the letter to Cibras on the 8th—Randolph despatches it, but the earl writes it. So with the disposal of the jewels in the apartment on the 9th. There had been some burglaries in the neighbourhood, and the suspicion at once arises in the mind of the crude reasoner: Could Randolph—finding now that Cibras has "left the country," that, in fact, the tool he had expected to serve his ends has failed him—could he have thus brought those jewels there, and thus warned the servants of their presence, in the hope that the intelligence might so get abroad and lead to a burglary, in the course of which his father might lose his life? There are evidences, you know, tending to show that the burglary did actually at last take place, and the suspicion is, in view of that, by no means unreasonable. And yet, militating against it, is our knowledge that it was Lord Pharanx who "*chose*" to gather the jewels round him; that it was in his presence that Randolph drew the attention of the servant to them. In the matter, at least, of the little political comedy the son seems to have acted alone; but you surely cannot rid yourself of the impression that the radical speeches, the candidature, and the rest of it, formed all of them only a very elaborate, and withal clumsy, set of preliminaries to the *class*. Anything, to make the perspective, the sequence of *that* seem natural. But in the class, at any rate, we have the tacit acquiescence, or even the cooperation of Lord Pharanx. You have described the conspiracy of quiet which, for some reason or other, was imposed on the household; in that reign of silence the bang of a door, the fall of a plate, becomes a domestic tornado. But have you ever heard an agricultural labourer in clogs or heavy boots ascend a stair? The noise is terrible. The tramp of an army of them through the house and overhead, probably jabbering uncouthly together, would be insufferable. Yet Lord Pharanx seems to have made no objection; the novel institution is set up in his own mansion, in an unusual part of it, probably against his own principles; but we hear of no murmur from him. On the fatal day, too, the calm of the house is rudely broken by a considerable commotion in Randolph's room just overhead, caused by his preparation for "a journey to London." But the usual angry remonstrance is not forthcoming from the master. And do you not see how all this more than acquiescence of Lord Pharanx in the conduct of his son deprives that conduct of half its significance, its intrinsic suspiciousness?

'A hasty reasoner then would inevitably jump to the conclusion that Randolph was guilty of something—some evil intention—though of precisely what he would remain in doubt. But a more careful reasoner would pause: he would reflect that *as* the father was implicated in those acts, and *as* he was innocent of any such intention, so might possibly, even probably, be the son. This, I take it, has been the view of the officials, whose logic is probably far in advance of their imagination. But supposing we can adduce one act, undoubtedly actuated by evil intention on the part of Randolph—one act in which his father certainly did *not* participate— what follows next? Why, that we revert at once to the view of the hasty reasoner, and conclude that *all* the other acts in the same relation were actuated by the same evil motive; and having reached that point, we shall be unable longer to resist the conclusion that those of them in which his father had a share *might* have sprung from a like motive in *his* mind also; nor should the mere obvious impossibility of such a condition of things have even the very least influence on us, as thinkers, in causing us to close our mind against its logical possibility. I therefore make the inference, and pass on.

'Let us then see if we can by searching find out any absolutely certain deviation from right on the part of Randolph, in which we may be quite sure that his father was not an abettor. At eight on the night of the murder it is dark; there has been some snow, but the fall has ceased—how long before I know not, but so long that the interval becomes sufficiently appreciable to cause remark. Now the party going round the house come on two tracks of feet meeting at an angle. Of one track we are merely told that it was made by the small foot of a woman, and of it we know no more; of the other we learn that the feet were big and the boots clumsy, and, it is added, the marks were *half obliterated by the snow*. Two things then are clear: that the persons who made them came from different directions, and probably made them at different times. That, alone, by the way, may be a sufficient answer to your question as to whether Cibras was in collusion with the "burglars." But how does Randolph behave with reference to these tracks? Though he carries the lantern, he fails to perceive the first—the woman's—the discovery of which is made by a lad; but the second, half hidden in the snow, he notices readily enough, and at once points it out. He explains that burglars have been on the war-path. But examine his horror of surprise when he hears that the window is closed; when he sees the woman's bleeding fingers. He cannot help exclaiming, "My God! what has happened *now*?" But why "now"? The word cannot refer to his father's death, for that he knew, or guessed, beforehand, having heard the shot. Is it not rather the exclamation of a man whose schemes destiny has complicated? Besides, he should have *expected* to find the window closed: no one except himself, Lord Pharanx, and the workman, who was now dead, knew the secret of its construction; the burglars therefore, having entered and robbed the room, one of them, intending to go out, would press on the ledge, and the sash would fall on his hand with what result we know. The others would then either break the glass and so escape; or pass through the house; or remain prisoners. That immoderate surprise was therefore absurdly illogical, after seeing the burglar-track in the snow. But how, above all, do you account for Lord Pharanx's silence during and after the burglars' visit—if there was a visit? He was, you must remember, alive all that time; *they* did not kill him; certainly they did not shoot him, for the shot is heard after the snow has ceased to fall,—that is, after, long after, they have left, since it was the falling snow that had half obliterated their tracks; nor did they stab him, for to this Cibras confesses. Why then, being alive, and not gagged, did he give no token of the presence of his visitors? There were in fact no burglars at Orven Hall that night.'

'But the track!' I cried, 'the jewels found in the snow—the neckerchief!'

Zaleski smiled.

'Burglars,' he said, 'are plain, honest folk who have a just notion of the value of jewelry when they see it. They very properly regard it as mere foolish waste to drop precious stones about in the snow, and would refuse to company with a man weak enough to let fall his neckerchief on a cold night. The whole business of the burglars was a particularly inartistic trick, unworthy of its author. The mere facility with which Randolph discovered the buried jewels by the aid of a dim lantern, should have served as a hint to an educated police not afraid of facing the improbable. The jewels had been *put* there with the object of throwing suspicion on the imaginary burglars; with the same design the catch of the window had been wrenched off, the sash purposely left open, the track made, the valuables taken from Lord Pharanx's room. All this was deliberately done by some one—would it be rash to say at once by whom?

'Our suspicions having now lost their whole character of vagueness, and begun to lead us in a perfectly definite direction, let us examine the statements of Hester Dyett. Now, it is immediately comprehensible to me that the evidence of this woman at the public examinations was looked at askance. There can be no doubt that she is a poor specimen of humanity, an undesirable servant, a peering, hysterical caricature of a woman. Her statements, if formally recorded, were not believed; or if believed, were believed with only half the mind. No attempt was made to deduce anything from them. But for my part, if I wanted specially reliable evidence as to any matter of fact, it is precisely from such a being that I would seek it. Let me draw you a picture of that class of intellect. They have a greed for information, but the information, to satisfy them, must relate to actualities; they have no sympathy with fiction; it is from their impatience of what seems to be that springs their curiosity of what *is*. Clio is their muse, and she alone. Their whole lust is to gather knowledge through a hole, their whole faculty is to *peep*. But they are destitute of imagination, and do not lie; in their passion for realities they would esteem it a sacrilege to distort history. They make straight for the substantial, the indubitable. For this reason the Peniculi and Ergasili of Plautus seem to me far more true to nature than the character of Paul Pry in Jerrold's comedy. In one instance, indeed, the evidence of Hester Dyett appears, on the surface of it, to be quite false. She declares that she sees a round white object moving upward in the room. But the night being gloomy, her taper having gone out, she must have been standing in a dense darkness. How then could she see this object? Her evidence, it was argued, must be designedly false, or else (as she was in an ecstatic condition) the result of an excited fancy. But I have stated that such persons, nervous, neurotic even as they may be, are not fanciful. I therefore accept her evidence as true. And now, mark the consequence of that acceptance. I am driven to admit that there must, from some source, have been light in the room—a light faint enough, and diffused enough, to escape the notice of Hester herself. This being so, it must have proceeded from around, from below, or from above. There are no other alternatives. Around these was nothing but the darkness of the night; the room beneath, we know, was also in darkness. The light then came from the room above—from the mechanic class-room. But there is only one possible means by which the light from an upper can diffuse a lower room. It *must* be by a hole in the intermediate boards. We are thus driven to the discovery of an aperture of some sort in the flooring of that upper chamber. Given this, the mystery of the round white object "driven" upward disappears. We at once ask, why not *drawn* upward through the newly-discovered aperture by a string too small to be visible in the gloom? Assuredly it was drawn upward. And now having established a hole in the ceiling of the room in which Hester stands, is it unreasonable—even without further evidence—to suspect another in the flooring? But we actually have this further evidence. As she rushes to the door she falls, faints, and fractures the lower part of her leg. Had she fallen *over* some object, as you supposed, the result might have been a fracture also, but in a different part of the body; being where it was, it could only have been caused by placing the foot inadvertently in a hole while the rest of the body was in rapid motion. But this gives us an approximate idea of the *size* of the lower hole; it was at least big enough to admit the foot and lower leg, big enough therefore to admit that "good-sized ball of cotton" of which the woman speaks: and from the lower we are able to conjecture the size of the upper. But how comes it that these holes are nowhere mentioned in the evidence? It can only be because no one ever saw them. Yet the rooms must have been examined by the police, who, if they existed, must have seen them. They therefore did not exist: that is to say, the pieces which had been removed from the floorings had by that time been neatly replaced, and, in the case of the lower one, covered by the carpet, the removal of which had caused so much commotion in Randolph's room on the fatal day. Hester Dyett would have been able to notice and bring at least one of the apertures forward in evidence, but she fainted before she had time to find out the cause of her fall, and an hour later it was, you remember, Randolph himself who bore her from the room. But should not the aperture in the top floor have been observed by the class? Undoubtedly, if its position was in the open space in the middle of the room. But it was not observed, and therefore its position was not there, but in the only other place left—behind the apparatus used in demonstration. That then was *one* useful object which the apparatus—and with it the elaborate hypocrisy of class, and speeches, and candidature—served: it was made to act as a curtain, a screen. But had it no other purpose? That question we may answer when we know its name and its nature. And it is not beyond our powers to conjecture this with something like certainty. For the only "machines" possible to use in illustration of simple mechanics are the screw, the wedge, the scale, the lever, the wheel-and-axle, and Atwood's machine. The mathematical principles which any of these exemplify would, of course, be incomprehensible to such a class, but the first five most of all, and as there would naturally be some slight pretence of trying to make the learners understand, I therefore select the last; and this selection is justified when we remember that on the shot being heard, Randolph leans for support on the "machine," and stands in its shadow; but any of the others would be too small to throw any appreciable shadow, except one—the wheel, and-axle—and that one would hardly afford support to a tall man in the erect position. The Atwood's machine is therefore forced on us; as to its construction, it is, as you are aware, composed of two upright posts, with a cross-bar fitted with pulleys and strings, and is intended to show the motion of bodies acting under a constant force—the force of gravity, to wit. But now consider all the really glorious uses to which those same pulleys may be turned in lowering and lifting unobserved that "ball of cotton" through the two apertures, while the other strings with the weights attached are dangling before the dull eyes of the peasants. I need only point out that when the whole company trooped out of the room, Randolph was the last to leave it, and it is not now difficult to conjecture why.

'Of what, then, have we convicted Randolph? For one thing, we have shown that by marks of feet in the snow preparation was made beforehand for obscuring the cause of the earl's death. That death must therefore have been at least expected, foreknown. Thus we convict him of expecting it. And then, by an independent line of deduction, we can also discover the *means* by which he expected it to occur. It is clear that he did not expect it to occur when it did by the hand of Maude Cibras—for this is proved by his knowledge that she had left the neighbourhood, by his evidently genuine astonishment at the sight of the closed window, and, above all, by his truly morbid desire to establish a substantial, an irrefutable *alibi* for himself by going to Plymouth on the day when there was every reason to suppose she would do the deed—that is, on the 8th, the day of the earl's invitation. On the fatal night, indeed, the same morbid eagerness to build up a clear *alibi* is observable, for he surrounds himself with a cloud of witnesses in the upper chamber. But that, you will admit, is not nearly so perfect a one as a journey, say, to Plymouth would have been. Why then, expecting the death, did he not take some such journey? Obviously because on *this* occasion his personal presence was necessary. When, *in conjunction* with this, we recall the fact that during the intrigues with Cibras the lectures were discontinued, and again resumed immediately on her unlooked-for departure, we arrive at the conclusion that the means by which Lord Pharanx's death was expected to occur was the personal presence of Randolph *in conjunction* with the political speeches, the candidature, the class, the apparatus.

'But though he stands condemned of foreknowing, and being in some sort connected with, his father's death, I can nowhere find any indication of his having personally accomplished it, or even of his ever having had any such intention. The evidence is evidence of complicity—and nothing more. And yet—and yet—even of *this* we began by acquitting him unless we could discover, as I said, some strong, adequate, altogether irresistible motive for such complicity. Failing this, we ought to admit that at some point our argument has played us false, and led us into conclusions wholly at variance with our certain knowledge of the principles underlying human conduct in general. Let us therefore seek for such a motive—something deeper than personal enmity, stronger than personal ambition, *than the love of life itself!* And now, tell me, at the time of the occurrence of this mystery, was the whole past history of the House of Orven fully investigated?'

'Not to my knowledge,' I answered; 'in the papers there were, of course, sketches of the earl's career, but that I think was all.'

'Yet it cannot be that their past was unknown, but only that it was ignored. Long, I tell you, long and often, have I pondered on that history, and sought to trace with what ghastly secret has been pregnant the destiny, gloomful as Erebus and the murk of black-peplosed Nux, which for centuries has hung its pall over the men of this ill-fated house. Now at last I know. Dark, dark, and red with gore and horror is that history; down the silent corridors of the ages have these blood-soaked sons of Atreus fled shrieking before the pursuing talons of the dread Eumenides. The first earl received his patent in 1535 from the eighth Henry. Two years later, though noted as a rabid "king's man," he joined the Pilgrimage of Grace against his master, and was soon after executed, with Darcy and some other lords. His age was then fifty. His son, meantime, had served in the king's army under Norfolk. It is remarkable, by the way, that females have all along been rare in the family, and that in no instance has there been more than one son. The second earl, under the sixth Edward, suddenly threw up a civil post, hastened to the army, and fell at the age of forty at the battle of Pinkie in 1547. He was accompanied by his son. The third in 1557, under Mary, renounced the Catholic faith, to which, both before and since, the family have passionately clung, and suffered (at the age of forty) the last penalty. The fourth earl died naturally, but suddenly, in his bed at the age of fifty during the winter of 1566. At midnight *of the same day* he was laid in the grave by his son. This son was later on, in 1591, seen by *his* son to fall from a lofty balcony at Orven Hall, while walking in his sleep at high noonday. Then for some time nothing happens; but the eighth earl dies mysteriously in 1651 at the age of forty-five. A fire occurring in his room, he leapt from a window to escape the flames. Some of his limbs were thereby fractured, but he was in a fair way to recovery when there was a sudden relapse, soon ending in death. He was found to have been poisoned by *radix aconiti indica*, a rare Arabian poison not known in Europe at that time except to *savants*, and first mentioned by Acosta some months before. An attendant was accused and tried, but acquitted. The then son of the House was a Fellow of the newly-founded Royal Society, and author of a now-forgotten work on Toxicology, which, however, I have read. No suspicion, of course, fell on *him*.'

As Zaleski proceeded with this retrospect, I could not but ask myself with stirrings of the most genuine wonder, whether he could possess this intimate knowledge of *all* the great families of Europe! It was as if he had spent a part of his life in making special study of the history of the Orvens.

'In the same manner,' he went on, 'I could detail the annals of the family from that time to the present. But all through they have been marked by the same latent tragic elements; and I have said enough to show you that in each of the tragedies there was invariably something large, leering, something of which the mind demands explanation, but seeks in vain to find it. Now we need no longer seek. Destiny did not design that the last Lord of Orven should any more hide from the world the guilty secret of his race. It was the will of the gods—and he betrayed himself. "Return," he writes, "the beginning of the end is come." What end?

The end—perfectly well known to Randolph, needing no explanation for *him*. The old, old end, which in the ancient dim time led the first lord, loyal still at heart, to forsake his king; and another, still devout, to renounce his cherished faith, and yet another to set fire to the home of his ancestors. You have called the two last scions of the family "a proud and selfish pair of beings"; proud they were, and selfish too, but you are in error if you think their selfishness a personal one: on the contrary, they were singularly oblivious of self in the ordinary sense of the word. Theirs was the pride and the selfishness of *race*. What consideration, think you, other than the weal of his house, could induce Lord Randolph to take on himself the shame—for as such he certainly regards it—of a conversion to radicalism? He would, I am convinced, have *died* rather than make this pretence for merely personal ends. But he does it—and the reason? It is because he has received that awful summons from home; because "the end" is daily coming nearer, and it must not find him unprepared to meet it; it is because Lord Pharanx's senses are becoming *too* acute; because the clatter of the servants' knives at the other end of the house inflames him to madness; because his excited palate can no longer endure any food but the subtlest delicacies; because Hester Dyett is able from the posture in which he sits to conjecture that he is intoxicated; because, in fact, he is on the brink of the dreadful malady which physicians call "*General Paralysis of the Insane.*" You remember I took from your hands the newspaper containing the earl's letter to Cibras, in order to read it with my own eyes. I had my reasons, and I was justified. That letter contains three mistakes in spelling: "here" is printed "hear," "pass" appears as "pas," and "room" as "rume." Printers' errors, you say? But not so—one might be, two in that short paragraph could hardly be, three would be impossible. Search the whole paper through, and I think you will not find another. Let us reverence the theory of probabilities: the errors were the writer's, not the printer's. General Paralysis of the Insane is known to have this effect on the writing. It attacks its victims about the period of middle age—the age at which the deaths of all the Orvens who died mysteriously occurred. Finding then that the dire heritage of his race—the heritage of madness—is falling or fallen on him, he summons his son from India. On himself he passes sentence of death: it is the tradition of the family, the secret vow of self-destruction handed down through ages from father to son. But he must have aid: in these days it is difficult for a man to commit the suicidal act without detection—and if madness is a disgrace to the race, equally so is suicide. Besides, the family is to be enriched by the insurances on his life, and is thereby to be allied with royal blood; but the money will be lost if the suicide be detected. Randolph therefore returns and blossoms into a popular candidate.

'For a time he is led to abandon his original plans by the appearance of Maude Cibras; he hopes that *she* may be made to destroy the earl; but when she fails him, he recurs to it—recurs to it all suddenly, for Lord Pharanx's condition is rapidly becoming critical, patent to all eyes, could any eye see him—so much so that on the last day none of the servants are allowed to enter his room. We must therefore regard Cibras as a mere addendum to, an extraneous element in, the tragedy, not as an integral part of it. She did not shoot the noble lord, for she had no pistol; nor did Randolph, for he was at a distance from the bed of death, surrounded by witnesses; nor did the imaginary burglars. The earl therefore shot himself; and it was the small globular silver pistol, such as this'—here Zaleski drew a little embossed Venetian weapon from a drawer near him—'that appeared in the gloom to the excited Hester as a "ball of cotton," while it was being drawn upward by the Atwood's machine. But if the earl shot himself he could not have done so after being stabbed to the heart. Maude Cibras, therefore, stabbed a dead man. She would, of course, have ample time for stealing into the room and doing so after the shot was fired, and before the party reached the balcony window, on account of the delay on the stairs in procuring a second light; in going to the earl's door; in examining the tracks, and so on. But having stabbed a dead man, she is not guilty of murder. The message I just now sent by Ham was one addressed to the Home Secretary, telling him on no account to let Cibras die to-morrow. He well knows my name, and will hardly be silly enough to suppose me capable of using words without meaning. It will be perfectly easy to prove my conclusions, for the pieces removed from, and replaced in, the floorings can still be detected, if looked for; the pistol is still, no doubt, in Randolph's room, and its bore can be compared with the bullet found in Lord Pharanx's brain; above all, the jewels stolen by the "burglars" are still safe in some cabinet of the new earl, and may readily be discovered I therefore expect that the dénoûment will now take a somewhat different turn.'

That the dénoûment did take a different turn, and pretty strictly in accordance with Zaleski's forecast, is now matter of history, and the incidents, therefore, need no further comment from me in this place.

THE STONE OF THE EDMUNDSBURY MONKS

'Russia,' said Prince Zaleski to me one day, when I happened to be on a visit to him in his darksome sanctuary—'Russia may be regarded as land surrounded by ocean; that is to say, she is an island. In the same way, it is sheer gross irrelevancy to speak of *Britain* as an island, unless indeed the word be understood as a mere *modus loquendi* arising out of a rather poor geographical pleasantry. Britain, in reality, is a small continent. Near her—a little to the south-east—is situated the large island of Europe. Thus, the enlightened French traveller passing to these shores should commune within himself: "I now cross to the Mainland"; and retracing his steps: "I now return to the fragment rent by wrack and earthshock from the Mother-country." And this I say not in the way of paradox, but as the expression of a sober truth. I have in my mind merely the relative depth and extent—the *non-insularity*, in fact—of the impressions made by the several nations on the world. But this island of Europe has herself an island of her own: the name of it, Russia. She, of all lands, is the *terra incognita*, the unknown land; till quite lately she was more—she was the undiscovered, the unsuspected land. She *has* a literature, you know, and a history, and a language, and a purpose—but of all this the world has hardly so much as heard. Indeed, she, and not any Antarctic Sea whatever, is the real Ultima Thule of modern times, the true Island of Mystery.'

I reproduce these remarks of Zaleski here, not so much on account of the splendid tribute to my country contained in them, as because it ever seemed to me—and especially in connection with the incident I am about to recall—that in this respect at least he was a genuine son of Russia; if she is the Land, so truly was he the Man, of Mystery. I who knew him best alone knew that it was impossible to know him. He was a being little of the present: with one arm he embraced the whole past; the fingers of the other heaved on the vibrant pulse of the future. He seemed to me—I say it deliberately and with forethought—to possess the unparalleled power not merely of disentangling in retrospect, but of unravelling in prospect, and I have known him to relate *coming* events with unimaginable minuteness of precision. He was nothing if not superlative: his diatribes, now culminating in a very *extravaganza* of hyperbole—now sailing with loose wing through the downy, witched, Dutch cloud-heaps of some quaintest tramontane Nephelococcugia of thought—now laying down law of the Medes for the actual world of to-day—had oft-times the strange effect of bringing back to my mind the very singular old-epic epithet, [Greek: aenemoen]—*airy*—as applied to human thought. The mere grip of his memory was not simply extraordinary, it had in it a token, a hint, of the strange, the pythic—nay, the sibylline. And as his reflecting intellect, moreover, had all the lightness of foot of a chamois kid, unless you could contrive to follow each dazzlingly swift successive step, by the sum of which he attained his Alp-heights, he inevitably left on you the astounding, the confounding impression of mental omnipresence.

I had brought with me a certain document, a massive book bound in iron and leather, the diary of one Sir Jocelin Saul. This I had abstracted from a gentleman of my acquaintance, the head of a firm of inquiry agents in London, into whose hand, only the day before, it had come. A distant neighbour of Sir Jocelin, hearing by chance of his extremity, had invoked the assistance of this firm; but the aged baronet, being in a state of the utmost feebleness, terror, and indeed hysterical incoherence, had been able to utter no word in explanation of his condition or wishes, and, in silent abandonment, had merely handed the book to the agent.

A day or two after I had reached the desolate old mansion which the prince occupied, knowing that he might sometimes be induced to take an absorbing interest in questions that had proved themselves too profound, or too intricate, for ordinary solution, I asked him if he was willing to hear the details read out from the diary, and on his assenting, I proceeded to do so.

The brief narrative had reference to a very large and very valuable oval gem enclosed in the substance of a golden chalice, which chalice, in the monastery of St. Edmundsbury, had once lain centuries long within the Loculus, or inmost coffin, wherein reposed the body of St. Edmund. By pressing a hidden pivot, the cup (which was composed of two equal parts, connected by minute hinges) sprang open, and in a hollow space at the bottom was disclosed the gem. Sir Jocelin Saul, I may say, was lineally connected with—though, of course, not descendant from—that same Jocelin of Brakelonda, a brother of the Edmundsbury convent, who wrote the now so celebrated *Jocelini Chronica*: and the chalice had fallen into the possession of the family, seemingly at some time prior to the suppression of the monastery about 1537. On it was inscribed in old English characters of unknown date the words:

'Shulde this Ston stalen bee,

Or shuld it chaunges dre,

The Houss of Sawl and hys Hed anoon shal de.'

The stone itself was an intaglio, and had engraved on its surface the figure of a mythological animal, together with some nearly obliterated letters, of which the only ones remaining legible were those forming the word 'Has.' As a sure precaution against the loss of the gem, another cup had been made and engraved in an exactly similar manner, inside of which, to complete the delusion, another stone of the same size and cut, but of comparatively valueless material, had been placed.

Sir Jocelin Saul, a man of intense nervosity, lived his life alone in a remote old manor-house in Suffolk, his only companion being a person of Eastern origin, named Ul-Jabal. The baronet had consumed his vitality in the life-long attempt to sound the too fervid Maelstrom of Oriental research, and his mind had perhaps caught from his studies a tinge of their morbidness, their esotericism, their insanity. He had for some years past been engaged in the task of writing a stupendous work on Pre-Zoroastrian Theogonies, in which, it is to be supposed, Ul-Jabal acted somewhat in the capacity of secretary. But I will give *verbatim* the extracts from his diary:

'*June 11.*—This is my birthday. Seventy years ago exactly I slid from the belly of the great Dark into this Light and Life. My God! My God! it is briefer than the rage of an hour, fleeter than a mid-day trance. Ul-Jabal greeted me warmly—seemed to have been looking forward to it—and pointed out that seventy is of the fateful numbers, its only factors being seven, five, and two: the last denoting the duality of Birth and Death; five, Isolation; seven, Infinity. I informed him that this was also my father's birthday; and *his* father's; and repeated the oft-told tale of how the latter, just seventy years ago to-day, walking at twilight by the churchyard-wall, saw the figure of *himself* sitting on a grave-stone, and died five weeks later riving with the pangs of hell. Whereat the sceptic showed his two huge rows of teeth.

'What is his peculiar interest in the Edmundsbury chalice? On each successive birthday when the cup has been produced, he has asked me to show him the stone. Without any well-defined reason I have always declined, but to-day I yielded. He gazed long into its sky-blue depth, and then asked if I had no idea what the inscription "Has" meant. I informed him that it was one of the lost secrets of the world.

'*June 15.*—Some new element has entered into our existence here. Something threatens me. I hear the echo of a menace against my sanity and my life. It is as if the garment which enwraps me has grown too hot, too heavy for me. A notable drowsiness has settled on my brain—a drowsiness in which thought, though slow, is a thousandfold more fiery-vivid than ever. Oh, fair goddess of Reason, desert not me, thy chosen child!

'*June 18.*—Ul-Jabal?—that man is *the very Devil incarnate!*

'*June 19.*—So much for my bounty, all my munificence, to this poisonous worm. I picked him up on the heights of the Mountain of Lebanon, a cultured savage among cultured savages, and brought him here to be a prince of thought by my side. What though his plundered wealth—the debt I owe him—has saved me from a sort of ruin? Have not *I* instructed him in the sweet secret of Reason?

'I lay back on my bed in the lonely morning watches, my soul heavy as with the distilled essence of opiates, and in vivid vision knew that he had entered my apartment. In the twilight gloom his glittering rows of shark's teeth seemed impacted on my eyeball—I saw *them*, and nothing else. I was not aware when he vanished from the room. But at daybreak I crawled on hands and knees to the cabinet containing the chalice. The viperous murderer! He has stolen my gem, well knowing that with it he has stolen my life. The stone is gone—gone, my precious gem. A weakness overtook me, and I lay for many dreamless hours naked on the marble floor.

'Does the fool think to hide ought from my eyes? Can he imagine that I shall not recover my precious gem, my stone of Saul?

'*June 20.*—Ah, Ul-Jabal—my brave, my noble Son of the Prophet of God! He has replaced the stone! He would not slay an aged man. The yellow ray of his eye, it is but the gleam of the great thinker, not—not—the gleam of the assassin. Again, as I lay in semi-somnolence, I saw him enter my room, this time more distinctly. He went up to the cabinet. Shaking the chalice in the dawning, some hours after he had left, I heard with delight the rattle of the stone. I might have known he would replace it; I should not have doubted his clemency to a poor man like me. But the strange being!—he has taken the *other* stone from the *other* cup—a thing of little value to any man! Is Ul-Jabal mad or I?

'*June 21.*—Merciful Lord in Heaven! he has *not* replaced it—not *it*—but another instead of it. To-day I actually opened the chalice, and saw. He has put a stone there, the same in size, in cut, in engraving, but different in colour, in quality, in value—a stone I have never seen before. How has he obtained it—whence? I must brace myself to probe, to watch; I must turn myself into an eye to search this devil's-bosom. My life, this subtle, cunning Reason of mine, hangs in the balance.

'*June 22.*—Just now he offered me a cup of wine. I almost dashed it to the ground before him. But he looked steadfastly into my eye. I flinched: and drank—drank.

'Years ago, when, as I remember, we were at Balbec, I saw him one day make an almost tasteless preparation out of pure black nicotine, which in mere wanton lust he afterwards gave to some of the dwellers by the Caspian to drink. But the fiend would surely never dream of giving to me that browse of hell—to me an aged man, and a thinker, a seer.

'*June 23.*—The mysterious, the unfathomable Ul-Jabal! Once again, as I lay in heavy trance at midnight, has he invaded, calm and noiseless as a spirit, the sanctity of my chamber. Serene on the swaying air, which, radiant with soft beams of vermil and violet light, rocked me into variant visions of heaven, I reclined and regarded him unmoved. The man has replaced the valueless stone in the modern-made chalice, and has now stolen the false stone from the other, which *he himself* put there! In patience will I possess this my soul, and watch what shall betide. My eyes shall know no slumber!

'*June 24.*—No more—no more shall I drink wine from the hand of Ul-Jabal. My knees totter beneath the weight of my lean body. Daggers of lambent fever race through my brain incessant. Some fibrillary twitchings at the right angle of the mouth have also arrested my attention.

'*June 25.*—He has dared at open mid-day to enter my room. I watched him from an angle of the stairs pass along the corridor and open my door. But for the terrifying, death-boding thump, thump of my heart, I should have faced the traitor then, and told him that I knew all his treachery. Did I say that I had strange fibrillary twitchings at the right angle of my mouth, and a brain on fire? I have ceased to write my book—the more the pity for the world, not for me.

'*June 26.*—Marvellous to tell, the traitor, Ul-Jabal, has now placed *another* stone in the Edmundsbury chalice—also identical in nearly every respect with the original gem. This, then, was the object of his entry into my room yesterday. So that he has first stolen the real stone and replaced it by another; then he has stolen this other and replaced it by yet another; he has beside stolen the valueless stone from the modern chalice, and then replaced it. Surely a man gone rabid, a man gone dancing, foaming, raving mad!

'*June 28.*—I have now set myself to the task of recovering my jewel. It is here, and I shall find it. Life against life—and which is the best life, mine or this accursed Ishmaelite's? If need be, I will do murder—I, with this withered hand—so that I get back the heritage which is mine.

'To-day, when I thought he was wandering in the park, I stole into his room, locking the door on the inside. I trembled exceedingly, knowing that his eyes are in every place. I ransacked the chamber, dived among his clothes, but found no stone. One singular thing in a drawer I saw: a long, white beard, and a wig of long and snow-white hair. As I passed out of the chamber, lo, he stood face to face with me at the door in the passage. My heart gave one bound, and then seemed wholly to cease its travail. Oh, I must be sick unto death, weaker than a bruised reed! When I woke from my swoon he was supporting me in his arms. "Now," he said, grinning down at me, "now you have at last delivered all into my hands." He left me, and I saw him go into his room and lock the door upon himself. What is it I have delivered into the madman's hands?

'*July 1*.—Life against life—and his, the young, the stalwart, rather than mine, the mouldering, the sere. I love life. Not *yet* am I ready to weigh anchor, and reeve halliard, and turn my prow over the watery paths of the wine-brown Deeps. Oh no. Not yet. Let *him* die. Many and many are the days in which I shall yet see the light, walk, think. I am averse to end the number of my years: there is even a feeling in me at times that this worn body shall never, never taste of death. The chalice predicts indeed that I and my house shall end when the stone is lost—a mere fiction *at first*, an idler's dream *then*, but now—now—that the prophecy has stood so long a part of the reality of things, and a fact among facts—no longer fiction, but Adamant, stern as the very word of God. Do I not feel hourly since it has gone how the surges of life ebb, ebb ever lower in my heart? Nay, nay, but there is hope. I have here beside me an Arab blade of subtle Damascene steel, insinuous to pierce and to hew, with which in a street of Bethlehem I saw a Syrian's head cleft open—a gallant stroke! The edges of this I have made bright and white for a nuptial of blood.

'*July 2*.—I spent the whole of the last night in searching every nook and crack of the house, using a powerful magnifying lens. At times I thought Ul-Jabal was watching me, and would pounce out and murder me. Convulsive tremors shook my frame like earthquake. Ah me, I fear I am all too frail for this work. Yet dear is the love of life.

'*July 7*.—The last days I have passed in carefully searching the grounds, with the lens as before. Ul-Jabal constantly found pretexts for following me, and I am confident that every step I took was known to him. No sign anywhere of the grass having been disturbed. Yet my lands are wide, and I cannot be sure. The burden of this mighty task is greater than I can bear. I am weaker than a bruised reed. Shall I not slay my enemy, and make an end?

'*July 8*.—Ul-Jabal has been in my chamber again! I watched him through a crack in the panelling. His form was hidden by the bed, but I could see his hand reflected in the great mirror opposite the door. First, I cannot guess why, he moved to a point in front of the mirror the chair in which I sometimes sit. He then went to the box in which lie my few garments—and opened it. Ah, I have the stone—safe—safe! He fears my cunning, ancient eyes, and has hidden it in the one place where I would be least likely to seek it—*in my own trunk*! And yet I dread, most intensely I dread, to look.

'*July 9.*—The stone, alas, is not there! At the last moment he must have changed his purpose. Could his wondrous sensitiveness of intuition have made him feel that my eyes were looking in on him?

'*July 10.*—In the dead of night I knew that a stealthy foot had gone past my door. I rose and threw a mantle round me; I put on my head my cap of fur; I took the tempered blade in my hands; then crept out into the dark, and followed. Ul-Jabal carried a small lantern which revealed him to me. My feet were bare, but he wore felted slippers, which to my unfailing ear were not utterly noiseless. He descended the stairs to the bottom of the house, while I crouched behind him in the deepest gloom of the corners and walls. At the bottom he walked into the pantry: there stopped, and turned the lantern full in the direction of the spot where I stood; but so agilely did I slide behind a pillar, that he could not have seen me. In the pantry he lifted the trap-door, and descended still further into the vaults beneath the house. Ah, the vaults,—the long, the tortuous, the darksome vaults,—how had I forgotten them? Still I followed, rent by seismic shocks of terror. I had not forgotten the weapon: could I creep near enough, I felt that I might plunge it into the marrow of his back. He opened the iron door of the first vault and passed in. If I could lock him in?—but he held the key. On and on he wound his way, holding the lantern near the ground, his head bent down. The thought came to me *then*, that, had I but the courage, one swift sweep, and all were over. I crept closer, closer. Suddenly he turned round, and made a quick step in my direction. I saw his eyes, the murderous grin of his jaw. I know not if he saw me—thought forsook me. The weapon fell with clatter and clangor from my grasp, and in panic fright I fled with extended arms and the headlong swiftness of a stripling, through the black labyrinths of the caverns, through the vacant corridors of the house, till I reached my chamber, the door of which I had time to fasten on myself before I dropped, gasping, panting for very life, on the floor.

'*July 11.*—I had not the courage to see Ul-Jabal to-day. I have remained locked in my chamber all the time without food or water. My tongue cleaves to the roof of my mouth.

'*July 12.*—I took heart and crept downstairs. I met him in the study. He smiled on me, and I on him, as if nothing had happened between us. Oh, our old friendship, how it has turned into bitterest hate! I had taken the false stone from the Edmundsbury chalice and put it in the pocket of my brown gown, with the bold intention of showing it to him, and asking him if he knew aught of it. But when I faced him, my courage failed again. We drank together and ate together as in the old days of love.

'July 13.—I cannot think that I have not again imbibed some soporiferous drug. A great heaviness of sleep weighed on my brain till late in the day. When I woke my thoughts were in wild distraction, and a most peculiar condition of my skin held me fixed before the mirror. It is dry as parchment, and brown as the leaves of autumn.

'July 14.—Ul-Jabal is gone! And I am left a lonely, a desolate old man! He said, though I swore it was false, that I had grown to mistrust him! that I was hiding something from him! that he could live with me no more! No more, he said, should I see his face! The debt I owe him he would forgive. He has taken one small parcel with him,—and is gone!

'July 15.—Gone! gone! In mazeful dream I wander with uncovered head far and wide over my domain, seeking I know not what. The stone he has with him—the precious stone of Saul. I feel the life-surge ebbing, ebbing in my heart.'

Here the manuscript abruptly ended.

Prince Zaleski had listened as I read aloud, lying back on his Moorish couch and breathing slowly from his lips a heavy reddish vapour, which he imbibed from a very small, carved, bismuth pipette. His face, as far as I could see in the green-grey crepuscular atmosphere of the apartment, was expressionless. But when I had finished he turned fully round on me, and said:

'You perceive, I hope, the sinister meaning of all this?'

'*Has* it a meaning?'

Zaleski smiled.

'Can you doubt it? in the shape of a cloud, the pitch of a thrush's note, the *nuance* of a sea-shell you would find, had you only insight *enough*, inductive and deductive cunning *enough*, not only a meaning, but, I am convinced, a quite endless significance. Undoubtedly, in a human document of this kind, there is a meaning; and I may say at once that this meaning is entirely transparent to me. Pity only that you did not read the diary to me before.'

'Why?'

'Because we might, between us, have prevented a crime, and saved a life. The last entry in the diary was made on the 15th of July. What day is this?'

'This is the 20th.'

'Then I would wager a thousand to one that we are too late. There is still, however, the one chance left. The time is now seven o'clock: seven of the evening, I think, not of the morning; the houses of business in London are therefore closed. But why not send my man, Ham, with a letter by train to the private address of the person from whom you obtained the diary, telling him to hasten immediately to Sir Jocelin Saul, and on no consideration to leave his side for a moment? Ham would reach this person before midnight, and understanding that the matter was one of life and death, he would assuredly do your bidding.'

As I was writing the note suggested by Zaleski, I turned and asked him:

'From whom shall I say that the danger is to be expected—from the Indian?'

'From Ul-Jabal, yes; but by no means Indian—Persian.'

Profoundly impressed by this knowledge of detail derived from sources which had brought me no intelligence, I handed the note to the negro, telling him how to proceed, and instructing him before starting from the station to search all the procurable papers of the last few days, and to return in case he found in any of them a notice of the death of Sir Jocelin Saul. Then I resumed my seat by the side of Zaleski.

'As I have told you,' he said, 'I am fully convinced that our messenger has gone on a bootless errand. I believe you will find that what has really occurred is this: either yesterday, or the day before, Sir Jocelin was found by his servant—I imagine he had a servant, though no mention is made of any—lying on the marble floor of his chamber, dead. Near him, probably by his side, will be found a gem—an oval stone, white in colour—the same in fact which Ul-Jabal last placed in the Edmundsbury chalice. There will be no marks of violence—no trace of poison—the death will be found to be a perfectly natural one. Yet, in this case, a particularly wicked murder has been committed. There are, I assure you, to my positive knowledge forty-three—and in one island in the South Seas, forty-four—different methods of doing murder, any one of which would be entirely beyond the scope of the introspective agencies at the ordinary disposal of society.

'But let us bend our minds to the details of this matter. Let us ask first, *who* is this Ul-Jabal? I have said that he is a Persian, and of this there is abundant evidence in the narrative other than his mere name. Fragmentary as the document is, and not intended by the writer to afford the information, there is yet evidence of the religion of this man, of the particular sect of that religion to which he belonged, of his peculiar shade of colour, of the object of his stay at the manor-house of Saul, of the special tribe amongst whom he formerly lived. "What," he asks, when his greedy eyes first light on the long-desired gem, "what is the meaning of the inscription 'Has'"—the meaning which *he* so well knew. "One of the lost secrets of the world," replies the baronet. But I can hardly understand a learned Orientalist speaking in that way about what appears to me a very patent circumstance: it is clear that he never earnestly applied himself to the solution of the riddle, or else—what is more likely, in spite of his rather high-flown estimate of his own "Reason"—that his mind, and the mind of his ancestors, never was able to go farther back in time than the Edmundsbury Monks. But *they* did not make the stone, nor did they dig it from the depths of the earth in Suffolk—they got it from some one, and it is not difficult to say with certainty from whom. The stone, then, might have been engraved by that someone, or by the someone from whom *he* received it, and so on back into the dimnesses of time. And consider the character of the engraving—it consists of *a mythological animal*, and some words, of which the letters "Has" only are distinguishable. But the animal, at least, is pure Persian. The Persians, you know, were not only quite worthy competitors with the Hebrews, the Egyptians, and later on the Greeks, for excellence in the glyptic art, but this fact is remarkable, that in much the same way that the figure of the *scarabaeus* on an intaglio or cameo is a pretty infallible indication of an Egyptian hand, so is that of a priest or a grotesque animal a sure indication of a Persian. We may say, then, from that evidence alone—though there is more—that this gem was certainly Persian. And having reached that point, the mystery of "Has" vanishes: for we at once jump at the conclusion that that too is Persian. But Persian, you say, written in English characters? Yes, and it was precisely this fact that made its meaning one of what the baronet childishly calls "the lost secrets of the world": for every successive inquirer, believing it part of an English phrase, was thus hopelessly led astray in his investigation. "Has" is, in fact, part of the word "Hasn-us-Sabah," and the mere circumstance that some of it has been obliterated, while the figure of the mystic animal remains intact, shows that it was executed by one of a nation less skilled in the art of graving in precious stones than the Persians,—by a rude, mediaeval Englishman, in short,—the modern revival of the art owing its origin, of course, to the Medici of a later age. And of this Englishman—who either graved the stone himself, or got some one else to do it for him—do we know nothing? We know, at least, that he was certainly a fighter, probably a Norman baron, that on his arm he bore the cross of red, that he trod the sacred soil of Palestine. Perhaps, to prove this, I need hardly remind you who Hasn-us-Sabah was. It is enough if I say that he was greatly mixed up in the affairs of the Crusaders, lending his irresistible arms now to this side, now to that. He was the chief of the heterodox Mohammedan sect of the Assassins (this word, I believe, is actually derived from his name); imagined himself to be an incarnation of the Deity, and from his inaccessible rock-fortress of Alamut in the Elburz exercised a sinister influence on the intricate politics of the day. The Red Cross Knights called him Shaikh-ul-Jabal —the Old Man of the Mountains, that very nickname connecting him infallibly with the Ul-Jabal of our own times. Now three well-known facts occur to me in connection with this stone of the House of Saul: the first, that Saladin met in battle, and defeated, *and plundered*, in a certain place, on a certain day, this Hasn-us-Sabah, or one of his successors bearing the same name; the second, that about this time there was a cordial *rapprochement* between Saladin and Richard the Lion, and between the Infidels and the Christians generally, during which a free interchange of gems, then regarded as of deep mystic importance, took place—remember "The Talisman," and the "Lee Penny"; the third, that soon after the fighters of Richard, and then himself, returned to England, the Loculus or coffin of St. Edmund (as we are informed by the *Jocelini Chronica*) was *opened by the Abbot* at midnight, and the body of the martyr exposed. On such occasions it was customary to place gems and relics in the coffin, when it was again closed up. Now, the chalice with the stone was taken from this loculus; and is it possible not to believe that some knight, to whom it had been presented by one of Saladin's men, had in turn presented it to the monastery, first scratching uncouthly on its surface the name of Hasn to mark its semi-sacred origin, or perhaps bidding the monks to do so? But the Assassins, now called, I think, "al Hasani" or "Ismaili"—"that accursed *Ishmaelite*," the baronet exclaims in one place— still live, are still a flourishing sect impelled by fervid religious fanaticisms. And where think you is their chief place of settlement? Where, but on the heights of that same "Lebanon" on which Sir Jocelin "picked up" his too doubtful scribe and literary helper?

'It now becomes evident that Ul-Jabal was one of the sect of the Assassins, and that the object of his sojourn at the manor-house, of his financial help to the baronet, of his whole journey perhaps to England, was the recovery of the sacred gem which once glittered on the breast of the founder of his sect. In dread of spoiling all by over-rashness, he waits, perhaps for years, till he makes sure that the stone is the right one by seeing it with his own eyes, and learns the secret of the spring by which the chalice is opened. He then proceeds to steal it. So far all is clear enough. Now, this too is conceivable, that, intending to commit the theft, he had beforehand provided himself with another stone similar in size and shape—these being well known to him—to the other, in order to substitute it for the real stone, and so, for a time at least, escape detection. It is presumable that the chalice was not often *opened* by the baronet, and this would therefore have been a perfectly rational device on the part of Ul-Jabal. But assuming this to be his mode of thinking, how ludicrously absurd appears all the trouble he took to *engrave* the false stone in an exactly similar manner to the other. *That* could not help him in producing the deception, for that he did not contemplate the stone being *seen*, but only *heard* in the cup, is proved by the fact that he selected a stone of a different *colour*. This colour, as I shall afterwards show you, was that of a pale, brown-spotted stone. But we are met with something more extraordinary still when we come to the last stone, the white one—I shall prove that it was white—which Ul-Jabal placed in the cup. Is it possible that he had provided *two* substitutes, and that he had engraved these *two*, without object, in the same minutely careful manner? Your mind refuses to conceive it; and *having* done this, declines, in addition, to believe that he had prepared even one substitute; and I am fully in accord with you in this conclusion.

'We may say then that Ul-Jabal had not *prepared* any substitute; and it may be added that it was a thing altogether beyond the limits of the probable that he could *by chance* have possessed two old gems exactly similar in every detail down to the very half-obliterated letters of the word "Hasn-us-Sabah." I have now shown, you perceive, that he did not make them purposely, and that he did not possess them accidentally. Nor were they the baronet's, for we have his declaration that he had never seen them before. Whence then did the Persian obtain them? That point will immediately emerge into clearness, when we have sounded his motive for replacing the one false stone by the other, and, above all, for taking away the valueless stone, and then replacing it. And in order to lead you up to the comprehension of this motive, I begin by making the bold assertion that Ul-Jabal had not in his possession the real St. Edmundsbury stone at all.

'You are surprised; for you argue that if we are to take the baronet's evidence at all, we must take it in this particular also, and he positively asserts that he saw the Persian take the stone. It is true that there are indubitable signs of insanity in the document, but it is the insanity of a diseased mind manifesting itself by fantastic exaggeration of sentiment, rather than of a mind confiding to itself its own delusions as to matters of fact. There is therefore nothing so certain as that Ul-Jabal did steal the gem; but these two things are equally evident: that by some means or other it very soon passed out of his possession, and that when it had so passed, he, for his part, believed it to be in the possession of the baronet. "Now," he cries in triumph, one day as he catches Sir Jocelin in his room—"*now* you have delivered all into my hands." "All" what, Sir Jocelin wonders. "All," of course, meant the stone. He believes that the baronet has done precisely what the baronet afterwards believes that *he* has done—hidden away the stone in the most secret of all places, in his own apartment, to wit. The Persian, sure now at last of victory, accordingly hastens into his chamber, and "locks the door," in order, by an easy search, to secure his prize. When, moreover, the baronet is examining the house at night with his lens, he believes that Ul-Jabal is spying his movements; when he extends his operations to the park, the other finds pretexts to be near him. Ul-Jabal dogs his footsteps like a shadow. But supposing he had really had the jewel, and had deposited it in a place of perfect safety—such as, with or without lenses, the extensive grounds of the manor-house would certainly have afforded—his more reasonable *rôle* would have been that of unconscious *nonchalance*, rather than of agonised interest. But, in fact, he supposed the owner of the stone to be himself seeking a secure hiding-place for it, and is resolved at all costs on knowing the secret. And again in the vaults beneath the house Sir Jocelin reports that Ul-Jabal "holds the lantern near the ground, with his head bent down": can anything be better descriptive of the attitude of *search*? Yet each is so sure that the other possesses the gem, that neither is able to suspect that both are seekers.

'But, after all, there is far better evidence of the non-possession of the stone by the Persian than all this—and that is the murder of the baronet, for I can almost promise you that our messenger will return in a few minutes. Now, it seems to me that Ul-Jabal was not really murderous, averse rather to murder; thus the baronet is often in his power, swoons in his arms, lies under the influence of narcotics in semi-sleep while the Persian is in his room, and yet no injury is done him. Still, when the clear necessity to murder—the clear means of gaining the stone—presents itself to Ul-Jabal, he does not hesitate a moment—indeed, he has already made elaborate preparations for that very necessity. And when was it that this necessity presented itself? It was when the baronet put the false stone in the pocket of a loose gown for the purpose of confronting the Persian with it. But what kind of pocket? I think you will agree with me, that male garments, admitting of the designation "gown," have usually only outer pockets—large, square pockets, simply sewed on to the outside of the robe. But a stone of that size *must* have made such a pocket bulge outwards. Ul-Jabal must have noticed it. Never before has he been perfectly sure that the baronet carried the long-desired gem about on his body; but now at last he knows beyond all doubt. To obtain it, there are several courses open to him: he may rush there and then on the weak old man and tear the stone from him; he may ply him with narcotics, and extract it from the pocket during sleep. But in these there is a small chance of failure; there is a certainty of near or ultimate detection, pursuit—and this is a land of Law, swift and fairly sure. No, the old man must die: only thus—thus surely, and thus secretly—can the outraged dignity of Hasn-us-Sabah be appeased. On the very next day he leaves the house—no more shall the mistrustful baronet, who is "hiding something from him," see his face. He carries with him a small parcel. Let me tell you what was in that parcel: it contained the baronet's fur cap, one of his "brown gowns," and a snow-white beard and wig. Of the cap we can be sure; for from the fact that, on leaving his room at midnight to follow the Persian through the *house*, he put it on his head, I gather that he wore it habitually during all his waking hours; yet after Ul-

Jabal has left him he wanders *far and wide* "with uncovered head." Can you not picture the distracted old man seeking ever and anon with absent mind for his long-accustomed head-gear, and seeking in vain? Of the gown, too, we may be equally certain: for it was the procuring of this that led Ul-Jabal to the baronet's trunk; we now know that he did not go there to *hide* the stone, for he had it not to hide; nor to *seek* it, for he would be unable to believe the baronet childish enough to deposit it in so obvious a place. As for the wig and beard, they had been previously seen in his room. But before he leaves the house Ul-Jabal has one more work to do: once more the two eat and drink together as in "the old days of love"; once more the baronet is drunken with a deep sleep, and when he wakes, his skin is "brown as the leaves of autumn." That is the evidence of which I spake in the beginning as giving us a hint of the exact shade of the Oriental's colour—it was the yellowish-brown of a sered leaf. And now that the face of the baronet has been smeared with this indelible pigment, all is ready for the tragedy, and Ul-Jabal departs. He will return, but not immediately, for he will at least give the eyes of his victim time to grow accustomed to the change of colour in his face; nor will he tarry long, for there is no telling whether, or whither, the stone may not disappear from that outer pocket. I therefore surmise that the tragedy took place a day or two ago. I remembered the feebleness of the old man, his highly neurotic condition; I thought of those "fibrillary twitchings," indicating the onset of a well-known nervous disorder sure to end in sudden death; I recalled his belief that on account of the loss of the stone, in which he felt his life bound up, the chariot of death was urgent on his footsteps; I bore in mind his memory of his grandfather dying in agony just seventy years ago after seeing his own wraith by the churchyard-wall; I knew that such a man could not be struck by the sudden, the terrific shock of seeing *himself* sitting in the chair before the mirror (the chair, you remember, had been *placed* there by Ul-Jabal) without dropping down stone dead on the spot. I was thus able to predict the manner and place of the baronet's death—if he *be* dead. Beside him, I said, would probably be found a white stone. For Ul-Jabal, his ghastly impersonation ended, would hurry to the pocket, snatch out the stone, and finding it not the stone he sought, would in all likelihood dash it down, fly away from the corpse as if from plague, and, I hope, straightway go and—hang himself.'

It was at this point that the black mask of Ham framed itself between the python-skin tapestries of the doorway. I tore from him the paper, now two days old, which he held in his hand, and under the heading, 'Sudden death of a Baronet,' read a nearly exact account of the facts which Zaleski had been detailing to me.

'I can see by your face that I was not altogether at fault,' he said, with one of his musical laughs; 'but there still remains for us to discover whence Ul-Jabal obtained his two substitutes, his motive for exchanging one for the other, and for stealing the valueless gem; but, above all, we must find where the real stone was all the time that these two men so sedulously sought it, and where it now is. Now, let us turn our attention to this stone, and ask, first, what light does the inscription on the cup throw on its nature? The inscription assures us that if "this stone be stolen," or if it "chaunges dre," the House of Saul and its head "anoon" (i.e. anon, at once) shall die. "Dre," I may remind you, is an old English word, used, I think, by Burns, identical with the Saxon "*dreogan*," meaning to "suffer." So that the writer at least contemplated that the stone might "suffer changes." But what kind of changes—external or internal? External change—change of environment—is already provided for when he says, "shulde this Ston stalen bee"; "chaunges," therefore, in *his* mind, meant internal changes. But is such a thing possible for any precious stone, and for this one in particular? As to that, we might answer when we know the name of this one. It nowhere appears in the manuscript, and yet it is immediately discoverable. For it was a "sky-blue" stone; a sky-blue, sacred stone; a sky-blue, sacred, Persian stone. That at once gives us its name—it was a *turquoise*. But can the turquoise, to the certain knowledge of a mediaeval writer, "chaunges dre"? Let us turn for light to old Anselm de Boot: that is he in pig-skin on the shelf behind the bronze Hera.'

I handed the volume to Zaleski. He pointed to a passage which read as follows:

'Assuredly the turquoise doth possess a soul more intelligent than that of man. But we cannot be wholly sure of the presence of Angels in precious stones. I do rather opine that the evil spirit doth take up his abode therein, transforming himself into an angel of light, to the end that we put our trust not in God, but in the precious stone; and thus, perhaps, doth he deceive our spirits by the turquoise: for the turquoise is of two sorts: those which keep their colour, and those which lose it.'[1]

> [1]'Assurément la turquoise a une âme plus intelligente que l'âme de l'homme. Mais nous ne pouvons rien establir de certain touchant la presence des Anges dans les pierres precieuses. Mon jugement seroit plustot que le mauvais esprit, qui se transforme en Ange de lumiere se loge dans les pierres precieuses, à fin que l'on ne recoure pas à Dieu, mais que l'on repose sa creance dans la pierre precieuse; ainsi, peut-être, il deçoit nos esprits par la turquoise: car la turquoise est de deux sortes, les unes qui conservent leur couleur et les autres qui la perdent.' *Anselm de Boot*, Book

II.

'You thus see,' resumed Zaleski, 'that the turquoise was believed to have the property of changing its colour—a change which was universally supposed to indicate the fading away and death of its owner. The good De Boot, alas, believed this to be a property of too many other stones beside, like the Hebrews in respect of their urim and thummim; but in the case of the turquoise, at least, it is a well-authenticated natural phenomenon, and I have myself seen such a specimen. In some cases the change is a gradual process; in others it may occur suddenly within an hour, especially when the gem, long kept in the dark, is exposed to brilliant sunshine. I should say, however, that in this metamorphosis there is always an intermediate stage: the stone first changes from blue to a pale colour spotted with brown, and, lastly, to a pure white. Thus, Ul-Jabal having stolen the stone, finds that it is of the wrong colour, and soon after replaces it; he supposes that in the darkness he has selected the wrong chalice, and so takes the valueless stone from the other. This, too, he replaces, and, infinitely puzzled, makes yet another hopeless trial of the Edmundsbury chalice, and, again baffled, again replaces it, concluding now that the baronet has suspected his designs, and substituted a false stone for the real one. But after this last replacement, the stone assumes its final hue of white, and thus the baronet is led to think that two stones have been substituted by Ul-Jabal for his own invaluable gem. All this while the gem was lying serenely in its place in the chalice. And thus it came to pass that in the Manor-house of Saul there arose a somewhat considerable Ado about Nothing.'

For a moment Zaleski paused; then, turning round and laying his hand on the brown forehead of the mummy by his side, he said:

'My friend here could tell you, and he would, a fine tale of the immensely important part which jewels in all ages have played in human history, human religions, institutions, ideas. He flourished some five centuries before the Messiah, was a Memphian priest of Amsu, and, as the hieroglyphics on his coffin assure me, a prime favourite with one Queen Amyntas. Beneath these mouldering swaddlings of the grave a great ruby still cherishes its blood-guilty secret on the forefinger of his right hand. Most curious is it to reflect how in *all* lands, and at *all* times, precious minerals have been endowed by men with mystic virtues. The Persians, for instance, believed that spinelle and the garnet were harbingers of joy. Have you read the ancient Bishop of Rennes on the subject? Really, I almost think there must be some truth in all this. The instinct of universal man is rarely far at fault. Already you have a semi-comic "gold-cure" for alcoholism, and you have heard of the geophagism of certain African tribes. What if the scientist of the future be destined to discover that the diamond, and it alone, is a specific for cholera, that powdered rubellite cures fever, and the chryso-beryl gout? It would be in exact conformity with what I have hitherto observed of a general trend towards a certain inborn perverseness and whimsicality in Nature.'

Note.—As some proof of the fineness of intuition evidenced by Zaleski, as distinct from his more conspicuous powers of reasoning, I may here state that some years after the occurrence of the tragedy I have recorded above, the skeleton of a man was discovered in the vaults of the Manor-house of Saul. I have not the least doubt that it was the skeleton of Ul-Jabal. The teeth were very prominent. A rotten rope was found loosely knotted round the vertebrae of his neck.

THE S.S.

'Wohlgeborne, gesunde Kinder bringen viel mit....

'Wenn die Natur verabscheut, so spricht sie es laut aus: das Geschöpf, das falsch lebt, wird früh zerstört. Unfruchtbarkeit, kümmerliches Dasein, frühzeitiges Zerfallen, das sind ihre Flüche, die Kennzeichen ihrer Strenge.' GOETHE. [Footnote: 'Well-made, healthy children bring much into the world along with them....

'When Nature abhors, she speaks it aloud: the creature that lives with a false life is soon destroyed. Unfruitfulness, painful existence, early destruction, these are her curses, the tokens of her displeasure.']

[Greek: Argos de andron echaerothae outo, oste oi douloi auton eschon panta ta praegmata, archontes te kai diepontes, es ho epaebaesan hoi ton apolomenon paides.] HERODOTUS. [Footnote: 'And Argos was so depleted of Men (i.e. *after the battle with Cleomenes*) that the slaves usurped everything—ruling and disposing—until such time as the sons of the slain were grown up.']

To say that there are epidemics of suicide is to give expression to what is now a mere commonplace of knowledge. And so far are they from being of rare occurrence, that it has even been affirmed that every sensational case of *felo de se* published in the newspapers is sure to be followed by some others more obscure: their frequency, indeed, is out of all proportion with the *extent* of each particular outbreak. Sometimes, however, especially in villages and small townships, the wildfire madness becomes an all-involving passion, emulating in its fury the great plagues of history. Of such kind was the craze in Versailles in 1793, when about a quarter of the whole population perished by the scourge; while that at the *Hôtel des Invalides* in Paris was only a notable one of the many which have occurred during the present century. At such times it is as if the optic nerve of the mind throughout whole communities became distorted, till in the noseless and black-robed Reaper it discerned an angel of very loveliness. As a brimming maiden, out-worn by her virginity, yields half-fainting to the dear sick stress of her desire—with just such faintings, wanton fires, does the soul, over-taxed by the continence of living, yield voluntary to the grave, and adulterously make of Death its paramour.

'When she sees a bank

Stuck full of flowers, she, with a sigh, will tell

Her servants, what a pretty place it were

To bury lovers in; and make her maids

Pluck 'em, and strew her over like a corse.'

[Footnote: Beaumont and Fletcher: *The Maid's Tragedy*.]

The *mode* spreads—then rushes into rage: to breathe is to be obsolete: to wear the shroud becomes *comme il faut*, this cerecloth acquiring all the attractiveness and *éclat* of a wedding-garment. The coffin is not too strait for lawless nuptial bed; and the sweet clods of the valley will prove no barren bridegroom of a writhing progeny. There is, however, nothing specially mysterious in the operation of a pestilence of this nature: it is as conceivable, if not yet as explicable, as the contagion of cholera, mind being at least as sensitive to the touch of mind as body to that of body.

It was during the ever-memorable outbreak of this obscure malady in the year 1875 that I ventured to break in on the calm of that deep Silence in which, as in a mantle, my friend Prince Zaleski had wrapped himself. I wrote, in fact, to ask him what he thought of the epidemic. His answer was in the laconic words addressed to the Master in the house of woe at Bethany:

'Come and see.'

To this, however, he added in postscript: 'but what epidemic?'

I had momentarily lost sight of the fact that Zaleski had so absolutely cut himself off from the world, that he was not in the least likely to know anything even of the appalling series of events to which I had referred. And yet it is no exaggeration to say that those events had thrown the greater part of Europe into a state of consternation, and even confusion. In London, Manchester, Paris, and Berlin, especially the excitement was intense. On the Sunday preceding the writing of my note to Zaleski, I was present at a monster demonstration held in Hyde Park, in which the Government was held up on all hands to the popular derision and censure—for it will be remembered that to many minds the mysterious accompaniments of some of the deaths daily occurring conveyed a still darker significance than that implied in mere self-destruction, and seemed to point to a succession of purposeless and hideous murders. The demagogues, I must say, spoke with some wildness and incoherence. Many laid the blame at the door of the police, and urged that things would be different were they but placed under municipal, instead of under imperial, control. A thousand panaceas were invented, a thousand aimless censures passed. But the people listened with vacant ear. Never have I seen the populace so agitated, and yet so subdued, as with the sense of some impending doom. The glittering eye betrayed the excitement, the pallor of the cheek the doubt, the haunting *fear*. None felt himself quite safe; men recognised shuddering the grin of death in the air. To tingle with affright, and to know not why—that is the transcendentalism of terror. The threat of the cannon's mouth is trivial in its effect on the mind in comparison with the menace of a Shadow. It is the pestilence that walketh *by night* that is intolerable. As for myself, I confess to being pervaded with a nameless and numbing awe during all those weeks. And this feeling appeared to be general in the land. The journals had but one topic; the party organs threw politics to the winds. I heard that on the Stock Exchange, as in the Paris *Bourse*, business decreased to a minimum. In Parliament the work of law-threshing practically ceased, and the time of Ministers was nightly spent in answering volumes of angry 'Questions,' and in facing motion after motion for the 'adjournment' of the House.

It was in the midst of all this commotion that I received Prince Zaleski's brief 'Come and see.' I was flattered and pleased: flattered, because I suspected that to me alone, of all men, would such an invitation, coming from him, be addressed; and pleased, because many a time in the midst of the noisy city street and the garish, dusty world, had the thought of that vast mansion, that dim and silent chamber, flooded my mind with a drowsy sense of the romantic, till, from very excess of melancholy sweetness in the picture, I was fain to close my eyes. I avow that that lonesome room—gloomy in its lunar bath of soft perfumed light—shrouded in the sullen voluptuousness of plushy, narcotic-breathing draperies—pervaded by the mysterious spirit of its brooding occupant—grew more and more on my fantasy, till the remembrance had for me all the cool refreshment shed by a midsummer-night's dream in the dewy deeps of some Perrhoebian grove of cornel and lotos and ruby stars of the asphodel. It was, therefore, in all haste that I set out to share for a time in the solitude of my friend.

Zaleski's reception of me was most cordial; immediately on my entrance into his sanctum he broke into a perfect torrent of wild, enthusiastic words, telling me with a kind of rapture, that he was just then laboriously engaged in co-ordinating to one of the calculi certain new properties he had discovered in the parabola, adding with infinite gusto his 'firm' belief that the ancient Assyrians were acquainted with all our modern notions respecting the parabola itself, the projection of bodies in general, and of the heavenly bodies in particular; and must, moreover, from certain inferences of his own in connection with the Winged Circle, have been conversant with the fact that light is not an ether, but only the vibration of an ether. He then galloped on to suggest that I should at once take part with him in his investigations, and commented on the timeliness of my visit. I, on my part, was anxious for his opinion on other and far weightier matters than the concerns of the Assyrians, and intimated as much to him. But for two days he was firm in his tacit refusal to listen to my story; and, concluding that he was disinclined to undergo the agony of unrest with which he was always tormented by any mystery which momentarily baffled him, I was, of course, forced to hold my peace. On the third day, however, of his own accord he asked me to what epidemic I had referred. I then detailed to him some of the strange events which were agitating the mind of the outside world. From the very first he was interested: later on that interest grew into a passion, a greedy soul-consuming quest after the truth, the intensity of which was such at last as to move me even to pity.

I may as well here restate the facts as I communicated them to Zaleski. The concatenation of incidents, it will be remembered, started with the extraordinary death of that eminent man of science, Professor Schleschinger, consulting laryngologist to the Charité Hospital in Berlin. The professor, a man of great age, was on the point of contracting his third marriage with the beautiful and accomplished daughter of the Herr Geheimrath Otto von Friedrich. The contemplated union, which was entirely one of those *mariages de convenance* so common in good society, sprang out of the professor's ardent desire to leave behind him a direct heir to his very considerable wealth. By his first two marriages, indeed, he had had large families, and was at this very time surrounded by quite an army of little grandchildren, from whom (all his direct descendants being dead) he might have been content to select his heir; but the old German prejudices in these matters are strong, and he still hoped to be represented on his decease by a son of his own. To this whim the charming Ottilie was marked by her parents as the victim. The wedding, however, had been postponed owing to a slight illness of the veteran scientist, and just as he was on the point of final recovery from it, death intervened to prevent altogether the execution of his design. Never did death of man create a profounder sensation; *never was death of man followed by consequences more terrible.* The *Residenz* of the scientist was a stately mansion near the University in the *Unter den Linden* boulevard, that is to say, in the most fashionable *Quartier* of Berlin. His bedroom from a considerable height looked out on a small back garden, and in this room he had been engaged in conversation with his colleague and medical attendant, Dr. Johann Hofmeier, to a late hour of the night. During all this time he seemed cheerful, and spoke quite lucidly on various topics. In particular, he exhibited to his colleague a curious strip of what looked like ancient papyrus, on which were traced certain grotesque and apparently meaningless figures. This, he said, he had found some days before on the bed of a poor woman in one of the horribly low quarters that surround Berlin, on whom he had had occasion to make a *post-mortem* examination. The woman had suffered from partial paralysis. She had a small young family, none of whom, however, could give any account of the slip, except one little girl, who declared that she had taken it 'from her mother's mouth' after death. The slip was soiled, and had a fragrant smell, as though it had been smeared with honey. The professor added that all through his illness he had been employing himself by examining these figures. He was convinced, he said, that they contained some archaeological significance; but, in any case, he ceased not to ask himself how came a slip of papyrus to be found in such a situation,—on the bed of a dead Berlinerin of the poorest class? The story of its being taken from the *mouth* of the woman was, of course, unbelievable. The whole incident seemed to puzzle, while it amused him; seemed to appeal to the instinct—so strong in him—to investigate, to probe. For days, he declared, he had been endeavouring, in vain, to make anything of the figures. Dr. Hofmeier, too, examined the slip, but inclined to believe that the figures—rude and uncouth as they were— were only such as might be drawn by any school-boy in an idle moment. They consisted merely of a man and a woman seated on a bench, with what looked like an ornamental border running round them. After a pleasant evening's scientific gossip, Dr. Hofmeier, a little after midnight, took his departure from the bed-side. An hour later the servants were roused from sleep by one deep, raucous cry proceeding from the professor's room. They hastened to his door; it was locked on the inside; all was still within. No answer coming to their calls, the door was broken in. They found their master lying calm and dead on his bed. A window of the room was open, but there was nothing to show that any one had entered it. Dr. Hofmeier was sent for, and was soon on the scene. After examining the body, he failed to find anything to account for the sudden demise of his old friend and chief. One observation, however, had the effect of causing him to tingle with horror. On his entrance he had noticed, lying on the side of the bed, the piece of papyrus with which the professor had been toying in the earlier part of the day, and had removed it. But, as he was on the point of leaving the room, he happened to approach the corpse once more, and bending over it, noticed that the lips and teeth were slightly parted. Drawing open the now stiffened jaws, he found—to his amazement, to his stupefaction—that, neatly folded beneath the dead tongue, lay just such another piece of papyrus as that which he had removed from the bed. He drew it out—it was clammy. He put it to his nose,—it exhaled the fragrance of honey. He opened it,—it was covered by figures. He compared them with the figures on the other slip,—they were just so similar as two draughtsmen hastily copying from a common model would make them. The doctor was unnerved: he hurried homeward, and immediately submitted the honey on the papyrus to a rigorous chemical analysis: he suspected poison—a subtle poison—as the means of a suicide, grotesquely, insanely accomplished. He found the fluid to be perfectly innocuous,—pure honey, and nothing more.

The next day Germany thrilled with the news that Professor Schleschinger had destroyed himself. For suicide, however, some of the papers substituted murder, though of neither was there an atom of actual proof. On the day following, three persons died by their own hands in Berlin, of whom two were young members of the medical profession; on the day following that, the number rose to nineteen, Hamburg, Dresden, and Aachen joining in the frenzied death-dance; within three weeks from the night on which Professor Schleschinger met his unaccountable end, eight thousand persons in Germany, France, and Great Britain, died in that startlingly sudden and secret manner which we call 'tragic', many of them obviously by their own hands, many, in what seemed the servility of a fatal imitativeness, with figured, honey-smeared slips of papyrus beneath their tongues. Even now—now, after years—I thrill intensely to recall the dread remembrance; but to live through it, to breathe daily the mawkish, miasmatic atmosphere, all vapid with the suffocating death—ah, it was terror too deep, nausea too foul, for mortal bearing. Novalis has somewhere hinted at the possibility (or the desirability) of a simultaneous suicide and voluntary return by the whole human family into the sweet bosom of our ancient Father—I half expected it was coming, had come, *then*. It was as if the old, good-easy, meek-eyed man of science, dying, had left his effectual curse on all the world, and had thereby converted civilisation into one omnivorous grave, one universal charnel-house. I spent several days in reading out to Zaleski accounts of particular deaths as they had occurred. He seemed never to tire of listening, lying back for the most part on the silver-cushioned couch, and wearing an inscrutable mask. Sometimes he rose and paced the carpet with noiseless foot-fall, his steps increasing to the swaying, uneven velocity of an animal in confinement as a passage here or there attracted him, and then subsiding into their slow regularity again. At any interruption in the reading, he would instantly turn to me with a certain impatience, and implore me to proceed; and when our stock of matter failed, he broke out into actual anger that I had not brought more with me. Henceforth the negro, Ham, using my trap, daily took a double journey—one before sunrise, and one at dusk—to the nearest townlet, from which he would return loaded with newspapers. With unimaginable eagerness did both Zaleski and I seize, morning after morning, and evening after evening, on these budgets, to gloat for long hours over the ever-lengthening tale of death. As for him, sleep forsook him. He was a man of small reasonableness, scorning the limitations of human capacity; his palate brooked no meat when his brain was headlong in the chase; even the mild narcotics which were now his food and drink seemed to lose something of their power to mollify, to curb him. Often rising from slumber in what I took to be the dead of night—though of day or night there could be small certainty in that dim dwelling—I would peep into the domed chamber, and see him there under the livid-green light of the censer, the leaden smoke issuing from his lips, his eyes fixed unweariedly on a square piece of ebony which rested on the coffin of the mummy near him. On this ebony he had pasted side by side several woodcuts—snipped from the newspapers—of the figures traced on the pieces of papyrus found in the mouths of the dead. I could see, as time passed, that he was concentrating all his powers on these figures; for the details of the deaths themselves were all of a dreary sameness, offering few salient points for investigation. In those cases where the suicide had left behind him clear evidence of the means by which he had committed the act, there was nothing to investigate; the others—rich and poor alike, peer and peasant—trooped out by thousands on the far journey, without leaving the faintest footprint to mark the road by which they had gone.

This was perhaps the reason that, after a time, Zaleski discarded the newspapers, leaving their perusal to me, and turned his attention exclusively to the ebon tablet. Knowing as I full well did the daring and success of his past spiritual adventures,—the subtlety, the imagination, the imperial grip of his intellect,—I did not at all doubt that his choice was wise, and would in the end be justified. These woodcuts—now so notorious—were all exactly similar in design, though minutely differing here and there in drawing. The following is a facsimile of one of them taken by me at random:

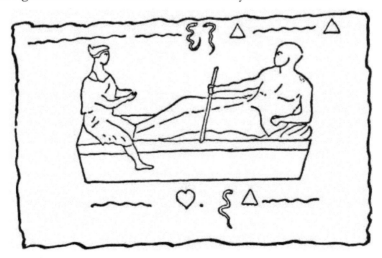

The time passed. It now began to be a grief to me to see the turgid pallor that gradually overspread the always ashen countenance of Zaleski; I grew to consider the ravaging life that glared and blazed in his sunken eye as too volcanic, demonic, to be canny: the mystery, I decided at last—if mystery there were—was too deep, too dark, for him. Hence perhaps it was, that I now absented myself more and more from him in the adjoining room in which I slept. There one day I sat reading over the latest list of horrors, when I heard a loud cry from the vaulted chamber. I rushed to the door and beheld him standing, gazing with wild eyes at the ebon tablet held straight out in front of him.

'By Heaven!' he cried, stamping savagely with his foot. 'By Heaven! Then I certainly *am* a fool! *It is the staff of Phaebus in the hand of Hermes!*'

I hastened to him. 'Tell me,' I said, 'have you discovered anything?'

'It is possible.'

'And has there really been foul play—murder—in any of these deaths?'

'Of that, at least, I was certain from the first.'

'Great God!' I exclaimed, 'could any son of man so convert himself into a fiend, a beast of the wilderness....'

'You judge precisely in the manner of the multitude,' he answered somewhat petulantly. 'Illegal murder is always a mistake, but not necessarily a crime. Remember Corday. But in cases where the murder of one is really fiendish, why is it qualitatively less fiendish than the murder of many? On the other hand, had Brutus slain a thousand Caesars—each act involving an additional exhibition of the sublimest self-suppression—he might well have taken rank as a saint in heaven.'

Failing for the moment to see the drift or the connection of the argument, I contented myself with waiting events. For the rest of that day and the next Zaleski seemed to have dismissed the matter of the tragedies from his mind, and entered calmly on his former studies. He no longer consulted the news, or examined the figures on the tablet. The papers, however, still arrived daily, and of these he soon afterwards laid several before me, pointing, with a curious smile, to a small paragraph in each. These all appeared in the advertisement columns, were worded alike, and read as follows:

'A true son of Lycurgus, *having news*, desires to know the *time* and *place* of the next meeting of his Phyle. Address Zaleski, at R---- Abbey, in the county of M----.'

I gazed in mute alternation at the advertisement and at him. I may here stop to make mention of a very remarkable sensation which my association with him occasionally produced in me. I felt it with intense, with unpleasant, with irritating keenness at this moment. It was the sensation of being borne aloft—aloft—by a force external to myself—such a sensation as might possibly tingle through an earthworm when lifted into illimitable airy heights by the strongly-daring pinions of an eagle. It was the feeling of being hurried out beyond one's depth—caught and whiffed away by the all-compelling sweep of some rabid vigour into a new, foreign element. Something akin I have experienced in an 'express' as it raged with me—winged, rocking, ecstatic, shrilling a dragon Aha!—round a too narrow curve. It was a sensation very far from agreeable.

'To that,' he said, pointing to the paragraph, 'we may, I think, shortly expect an answer. Let us only hope that when it comes it may be immediately intelligible.'

We waited throughout the whole of that day and night, hiding our eagerness under the pretence of absorption in our books. If by chance I fell into an uneasy doze, I found him on waking ever watchful, and poring over the great tome before him. About the time, however, when, could we have seen it, the first grey of dawn must have been peeping over the land, his impatience again became painful to witness; he rose and paced the room, muttering occasionally to himself. This only ceased, when, hours later, Ham entered the room with an envelope in his hand. Zaleski seized it—tore it open—ran his eye over the contents—and dashed it to the ground with an oath.

'Curse it!' he groaned. 'Ah, curse it! unintelligible—every syllable of it!'

I picked up the missive and examined it. It was a slip of papyrus covered with the design now so hideously familiar, except only that the two central figures were wanting. At the bottom was written the date of the 15th of November—it was then the morning of the 12th—and the name 'Morris.' The whole, therefore, presented the following appearance:

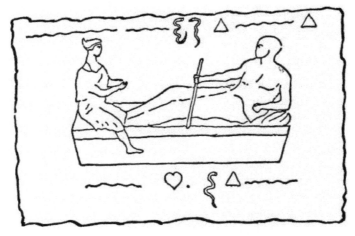

My eyes were now heavy with sleep, every sense half-drunken with the vapourlike atmosphere of the room, so that, having abandoned something of hope, I tottered willingly to my bed, and fell into a profound slumber, which lasted till what must have been the time of the gathering in of the shades of night. I then rose. Missing Zaleski, I sought through all the chambers for him. He was nowhere to be seen. The negro informed me with an affectionate and anxious tremor in the voice that his master had left the rooms some hours before, but had said nothing to him. I ordered the man to descend and look into the sacristy of the small chapel wherein I had deposited my *calèche*, and in the field behind, where my horse should be. He returned with the news that both had disappeared. Zaleski, I then concluded, had undoubtedly departed on a journey.

I was deeply touched by the demeanour of Ham as the hours went by. He wandered stealthily about the rooms like a lost being. It was like matter sighing after, weeping over, spirit. Prince Zaleski had never before withdrawn himself from the *surveillance* of this sturdy watchman, and his disappearance now was like a convulsion in their little cosmos. Ham implored me repeatedly, if I could, to throw some light on the meaning of this catastrophe. But I too was in the dark. The Titanic frame of the Ethiopian trembled with emotion as in broken, childish words he told me that he felt instinctively the approach of some great danger to the person of his master. So a day passed away, and then another. On the next he roused me from sleep to hand me a letter which, on opening, I found to be from Zaleski. It was hastily scribbled in pencil, dated 'London, Nov. 14th,' and ran thus:

'For my body—should I not return by Friday night—you will, no doubt, be good enough to make search. *Descend* the river, keeping constantly to the left; consult the papyrus; and stop at the *Descensus Aesopi*. Seek diligently, and you will find. For the rest, you know my fancy for cremation: take me, if you will, to the crematorium of *Père-Lachaise*. My whole fortune I decree to Ham, the Lybian.'

Ham was all for knowing the contents of this letter, but I refused to communicate a word of it. I was dazed, I was more than ever perplexed, I was appalled by the frenzy of Zaleski. Friday night! It was then Thursday morning. And I was expected to wait through the dreary interval uncertain, agonised, inactive! I was offended with my friend; his conduct bore the interpretation of mental distraction. The leaden hours passed all oppressively while I sought to appease the keenness of my unrest with the anodyne of drugged sleep. On the next morning, however, another letter— a rather massive one—reached me. The covering was directed in the writing of Zaleski, but on it he had scribbled the words: 'This need not be opened unless I fail to reappear before Saturday.' I therefore laid the packet aside unread.

I waited all through Friday, resolved that at six o'clock, if nothing happened, I should make some sort of effort. But from six I remained, with eyes strained towards the doorway, until ten. I was so utterly at a loss, my ingenuity was so entirely baffled by the situation, that I could devise no course of action which did not immediately appear absurd. But at midnight I sprang up—no longer would I endure the carking suspense. I seized a taper, and passed through the door-way. I had not proceeded far, however, when my light was extinguished. Then I remembered with a shudder that I should have to pass through the whole vast length of the building in order to gain an exit. It was an all but hopeless task in the profound darkness to thread my way through the labyrinth of halls and corridors, of tumble-down stairs, of bat-haunted vaults, of purposeless angles and involutions; but I proceeded with something of a blind obstinacy, groping my way with arms held out before me. In this manner I had wandered on for perhaps a quarter of an hour, when my fingers came into distinct momentary contact with what felt like cold and humid human flesh. I shrank back, unnerved as I already was, with a murmur of affright.

'Zaleski?' I whispered with bated breath.

Intently as I strained my ears, I could detect no reply. The hairs of my head, catching terror from my fancies, erected themselves.

Again I advanced, and again I became aware of the sensation of contact. With a quick movement I passed my hand upward and downward.

It was indeed he. He was half-reclining, half-standing against a wall of the chamber: that he was not dead, I at once knew by his uneasy breathing.

Indeed, when, having chafed his hands for some time, I tried to rouse him, he quickly recovered himself, and muttered: 'I fainted; I want sleep—only sleep.' I bore him back to the lighted room, assisted by Ham in the latter part of the journey. Ham's ecstasies were infinite; he had hardly hoped to see his master's face again. His garments being wet and soiled, the negro divested him of them, and dressed him in a tightly-fitting scarlet robe of Babylonish pattern, reaching to the feet, but leaving the lower neck and forearm bare, and girt round the stomach by a broad gold-orphreyed *ceinture*. With all the tenderness of a woman, the man stretched his master thus arrayed on the couch. Here he kept an Argus guard while Zaleski, in one deep unbroken slumber of a night and a day, reposed before him. When at last the sleeper woke, in his eye,—full of divine instinct,—flitted the wonted falchion-flash of the whetted, two-edged intellect; the secret, austere, self-conscious smile of triumph curved his lip; not a trace of pain or fatigue remained. After a substantial meal on nuts, autumn fruits, and wine of Samos, he resumed his place on the couch; and I sat by his side to hear the story of his wandering. He said:

'We have, Shiel, had before us a very remarkable series of murders, and a very remarkable series of suicides. Were they in any way connected? To this extent, I think—that the mysterious, the unparalleled nature of the murders gave rise to a morbid condition in the public mind, which in turn resulted in the epidemic of suicide. But though such an epidemic has its origin in the instinct of imitation so common in men, you must not suppose that the mental process is a *conscious* one. A person feels an impulse to go and do, and is not aware that at bottom it is only an impulse to go and do *likewise*. He would indeed repudiate such an assumption. Thus one man destroys himself, and another imitates him—but whereas the former uses a pistol, the latter uses a rope. It is rather absurd, therefore, to imagine that in any of those cases in which the slip of papyrus has been found in the mouth after death, the cause of death has been the slavish imitativeness of the suicidal mania,—for this, as I say, is never *slavish*. The papyrus then—quite apart from the unmistakable evidences of suicide invariably left by each self-destroyer—affords us definite and certain means by which we can distinguish the two classes of deaths; and we are thus able to divide the total number into two nearly equal halves.

'But you start—you are troubled—you never heard or read of murder such as this, the simultaneous murder of thousands over wide areas of the face of the globe; here you feel is something outside your experience, deeper than your profoundest imaginings. To the question "by whom committed?" and "with what motive?" your mind can conceive no possible answer. And yet the answer must be, "by man, and for human motives,"—for the Angel of Death with flashing eye and flaming sword is himself long dead; and again we can say at once, by no *one* man, but by many, a cohort, an army of men; and again, by no *common* men, but by men hellish (or heavenly) in cunning, in resource, in strength and unity of purpose; men laughing to scorn the flimsy prophylactics of society, separated by an infinity of self-confidence and spiritual integrity from the ordinary easily-crushed criminal of our days.

'This much at least I was able to discover from the first; and immediately I set myself to the detection of motive by a careful study of each case. This, too, in due time, became clear to me,—but to motive it may perhaps be more convenient to refer later on. What next engaged my attention was the figures on the papyrus, and devoutly did I hope that by their solution I might be able to arrive at some more exact knowledge of the mystery.

'The figures round the border first attracted me, and the mere *reading* of them gave me very little trouble. But I was convinced that behind their meaning thus read lay some deep esoteric significance; and this, almost to the last, I was utterly unable to fathom. You perceive that these border figures consist of waved lines of two different lengths, drawings of snakes, triangles looking like the Greek delta, and a heart-shaped object with a dot following it. These succeed one another in a certain definite order on all the slips. What, I asked myself, were these drawings meant to represent,—letters, numbers, things, or abstractions? This I was the more readily able to determine because I have often, in thinking over the shape of the Roman letter S, wondered whether it did not owe its convolute form to an attempt on the part of its inventor to make a picture of the *serpent;* S being the sibilant or hissing letter, and the serpent the hissing animal. This view, I fancy (though I am not sure), has escaped the philologists, but of course you know that all letters were originally *pictures of things,* and of what was S a picture, if not of the serpent? I therefore assumed, by way of trial, that the snakes in the diagram stood for a sibilant letter, that is, either C or S. And thence, supposing this to be the case, I deduced: firstly, that all the other figures stood for letters; and secondly, that they all appeared in the form of pictures of the things of which those letters were originally meant to be pictures. Thus the letter "m," one of the four "*liquid*" consonants, is, as we now write it, only a shortened form of a waved line; and as a waved line it was originally written, and was the character by which *a stream of running water* was represented in writing; indeed it only owes its name to the fact that when the lips are pressed together, and "m" uttered by a continuous effort, a certain resemblance to the murmur of running water is produced. The longer waved line in the diagram I therefore took to represent "m"; and it at once followed that the shorter meant "n," for no two letters of the commoner European alphabets differ only in length (as distinct from shape) except "m" and "n", and "w" and "v"; indeed, just as the French call "w" "double-ve," so very properly might "m" be called "double-en." But, in this case, the longer not being "w," the shorter could not be "v": it was therefore "n." And now there only remained the heart and the triangle. I was unable to think of any letter that could ever have been intended for the picture of a heart, but the triangle I knew to be the letter #A.# This was originally written without the cross-bar from prop to prop, and the two feet at the bottom of the props were not separated as now, but joined; so that the letter formed a true triangle. It was meant by the primitive man to be a picture of his primitive house, this house being, of course, hut-shaped, and consisting of a conical roof without walls. I had thus, with the exception of the heart, disentangled the whole, which then (leaving a space for the heart) read as follows: { ss

'mn {   anan ... san.'

{ cc

But 'c' before 'a' being never a sibilant (except in some few so-called 'Romance' languages), but a guttural, it was for the moment discarded; also as no word begins with the letters 'mn'—except 'mnemonics' and its fellows—I concluded that a vowel must be omitted between these letters, and thence that all vowels (except 'a') were omitted; again, as the double 's' can never come after 'n' I saw that either a vowel was omitted between the two 's's,' or that the first word ended after the first 's.' Thus I got

'm ns sanan... san,'

or, supplying the now quite obvious vowels,

'mens sana in... sano.'

The heart I now knew represented the word 'corpore,' the Latin word for 'heart' being 'cor,' and the dot—showing that the word as it stood was an abbreviation—conclusively proved every one of my deductions.

'So far all had gone flowingly. It was only when I came to consider the central figures that for many days I spent my strength in vain. You heard my exclamation of delight and astonishment when at last a ray of light pierced the gloom. At no time, indeed, was I wholly in the dark as to the *general* significance of these figures, for I saw at once their resemblance to the sepulchral reliefs of classical times. In case you are not minutely acquainted with the *technique* of these stones, I may as well show you one, which I myself removed from an old grave in Tarentum.'

He took from a niche a small piece of close-grained marble, about a foot square, and laid it before me. On one side it was exquisitely sculptured in relief.

'This,' he continued, 'is a typical example of the Greek grave-stone, and having seen one specimen you may be said to have seen almost all, for there is surprisingly little variety in the class. You will observe that the scene represents a man reclining on a couch; in his hand he holds a *patera*, or dish, filled with grapes and pomegranates, and beside him is a tripod bearing the viands from which he is banqueting. At his feet sits a woman—for the Greek lady never reclined at table. In addition to these two figures a horse's head, a dog, or a serpent may sometimes be seen; and these forms comprise the almost invariable pattern of all grave reliefs. Now, that this was the real model from which the figures on the papyrus were taken I could not doubt, when I considered the seemingly absurd fidelity with which in each murder the papyrus, smeared with honey, was placed under the tongue of the victim. I said to myself: it can only be that the assassins have bound themselves to the observance of a strict and narrow ritual from which no departure is under any circumstances permitted—perhaps for the sake of signalling the course of events to others at a distance. But what ritual? That question I was able to answer when I knew the answer to these others,— why *under the tongue*, and why *smeared with honey?* For no reason, except that the Greeks (not the Romans till very late in their history) always placed an *obolos*, or penny, beneath the tongue of the dead to pay his passage across the Stygian river of ghosts; for no reason, except that to these same Greeks honey was a sacred fluid, intimately associated in their minds with the mournful subject of Death; a fluid with which the bodies of the deceased were anointed, and sometimes—especially in Sparta and the Pelasgic South—embalmed; with which libations were poured to Hermes Psuchopompos, conductor of the dead to the regions of shade; with which offerings were made to all the chthonic deities, and the souls of the departed in general. You remember, for instance, the melancholy words of Helen addressed to Hermione in *Orestes:*

[Greek: Kai labe choas tasd'en cheroin komas t'emas

elthousa d'amphi ton Klutaimnaestras taphon

melikrat'aphes galaktos oinopon t'achnaen.]And so everywhere. The ritual then of the murderers was a *Greek* ritual, their cult a Greek cult— preferably, perhaps, a South Greek one, a Spartan one, for it was here that the highly conservative peoples of that region clung longest and fondliest to this semi-barbarous worship. This then being so, I was made all the more certain of my conjecture that the central figures on the papyrus were drawn from a Greek model.

'Here, however, I came to a standstill. I was infinitely puzzled by the rod in the man's hand. In none of the Greek grave-reliefs does any such thing as a rod make an appearance, except in one well-known example where the god Hermes—generally represented as carrying the *caduceus*, or staff, given him by Phoebus—appears leading a dead maiden to the land of night. But in every other example of which I am aware the sculpture represents a man *living*, not dead, banqueting *on earth*, not in Hades, by the side of his living companion. What then could be the significance of the staff in the hand of this living man? It was only after days of the hardest struggle, the cruellest suspense, that the thought flashed on me that the idea of Hermes leading away the dead female might, in this case, have been carried one step farther; that the male figure might be no living man, no man at all, but *Hermes himself* actually banqueting in Hades with the soul of his disembodied *protégée*! The thought filled me with a rapture I cannot describe, and you witnessed my excitement. But, at all events, I saw that this was a truly tremendous departure from Greek art and thought, to which in general the copyists seemed to cling so religiously. There must therefore be a reason, a strong reason, for vandalism such as this. And that, at any rate, it was no longer difficult to discover; for now I knew that the male figure was no mortal, but a god, a spirit, a DAEMON (in the Greek sense of the word); and the female figure I saw by the marked shortness of her drapery to be no Athenian, but a Spartan; no matron either, but a maiden, a lass, a LASSIE; and now I had forced on me lassie daemon, *Lacedaemon*.

'This then was the badge, the so carefully-buried badge, of this society of men. The only thing which still puzzled and confounded me at this stage was the startling circumstance that a *Greek* society should make use of a *Latin* motto. It was clear that either all my conclusions were totally wrong, or else the motto *mens sana in corpore sano* contained wrapped up in itself some acroamatic meaning which I found myself unable to penetrate, and which the authors had found no Greek motto capable of conveying. But at any rate, having found this much, my knowledge led me of itself one step further; for I perceived that, widely extended as were their operations, the society was necessarily in the main an *English,* or at least an English-speaking one—for of this the word "lassie" was plainly indicative: it was easy now to conjecture London, the monster-city in which all things lose themselves, as their head-quarters; and at this point in my investigations I despatched to the papers the advertisement you have seen.'

'But,' I exclaimed, 'even now I utterly fail to see by what mysterious processes of thought you arrived at the wording of the advertisement; even now it conveys no meaning to my mind.'

'That,' he replied,' will grow clear when we come to a right understanding of the baleful *motive* which inspired these men. I have already said that I was not long in discovering it. There was only one possible method of doing so—and that was, by all means, by any means, to find out some condition or other common to every one of the victims before death. It is true that I was unable to do this in some few cases, but where I failed, I was convinced that my failure was due to the insufficiency of the evidence at my disposal, rather than to the actual absence of the condition. Now, let us take almost any two cases you will, and seek for this common condition: let us take, for example, the first two that attracted the attention of the world—the poor woman of the slums of Berlin, and the celebrated man of science. Separated by as wide an interval as they are, we shall yet find, if we look closely, in each case the same pathetic tokens of the still uneliminated *striae* of our poor humanity. The woman is not an old woman, for she has a "small young" family, which, had she lived, might have been increased: notwithstanding which, she has suffered from hemiplegia, "partial paralysis." The professor, too, has had not one, but two, large families, and an "army of grand-children": but note well the startling, the hideous fact, that *every one of his children is dead!* The crude grave has gaped before the cock to suck in *every one* of those shrunk forms, so indigent of vital impulse, so pauper of civism, lust, so draughty, so vague, so lean—but not before they have had time to dower with the ah and wo of their infirmity a whole wretched "army of grand-children." And yet this man of wisdom is on the point, in his old age, of marrying once again, of producing for the good of his race still more of this poor human stuff. You see the lurid significance, the point of resemblance,—you see it? And, O heaven, is it not too sad? For me, I tell you, the whole business has a tragic pitifulness too deep for words. But this brings me to the discussion of a large matter. It would, for instance, be interesting to me to hear what you, a modern European, saturated with all the notions of your little day, what *you* consider the supreme, the all-important question for the nations of Europe at this moment. Am I far wrong in assuming that you would rattle off half a dozen of the moot points agitating rival factions in your own land, select one of them, and call that "the question of the hour"? I wish I could see as you see; I wish to God I did not see deeper. In order to lead you to my point, what, let me ask you, what *precisely* was it that ruined the old nations—that brought, say Rome, to her knees at last? Centralisation, you say, top-heavy imperialism, dilettante pessimism, the love of luxury. At bottom, believe me, it was not one of these high-sounding things—it was simply War; the sum total of the battles of centuries. But let me explain myself: this is a novel view to you, and you are perhaps unable to conceive how or why war was so fatal to the old world, because you see how little harmful it is to the new. If you collected in a promiscuous way a few millions of modern

Englishmen and slew them all simultaneously, what, think you, would be the effect from the point of view of the State? The effect, I conceive, would be indefinitely small, wonderfully transitory; there would, of course, be a momentary lacuna in the boiling surge: yet the womb of humanity is full of sap, and uberant; Ocean-tide, wooed of that Ilithyia whose breasts are many, would flow on, and the void would soon be filled. But the effect would only be thus insignificant, if, as I said, your millions were taken promiscuously (as in the modern army), not if they were *picked* men----in *that* case the loss (or gain) would be excessive, and permanent for all time. Now, the war-hosts of the ancient commonwealths—not dependent on the mechanical contrivances of the modern army—were necessarily composed of the very best men: the strong-boned, the heart-stout, the sound in wind and limb. Under these conditions the State shuddered through all her frame, thrilled adown every filament, at the death of a single one of her sons in the field. As only the feeble, the aged, bided at home, their number after each battle became larger *in proportion to the whole* than before. Thus the nation, more and more, with ever-increasing rapidity, declined in bodily, and of course spiritual, quality, until the *end* was reached, and Nature swallowed up the weaklings whole; and thus war, which to the modern state is at worst the blockhead and indecent *affaires d'honneur* of persons in office—and which, surely, before you and I die will cease altogether—was to the ancient a genuine and remorselessly fatal scourge.

'And now let me apply these facts to the Europe of our own time. We no longer have world-serious war—but in its place we have a scourge, the effect of which on the modern state is *precisely the same* as the effect of war on the ancient, only,—in the end,—far more destructive, far more subtle, sure, horrible, disgusting. The name of this pestilence is Medical Science. Yes, it is most true, shudder —shudder—as you will! Man's best friend turns to an asp in his bosom to sting him to the basest of deaths. The devastating growth of medical, and especially surgical, science—that, if you like, for us all, is "the question of the hour!" And what a question! of what surpassing importance, in the presence of which all other "questions" whatever dwindle into mere academic triviality. For just as the ancient State was wounded to the heart through the death of her healthy sons in the field, just so slowly, just so silently, is the modern receiving deadly hurt by the botching and tinkering of her unhealthy children. The net result is in each case the same—the altered ratio of the total amount of reproductive health to the total amount of reproductive disease. They recklessly spent their best; we sedulously conserve our worst; and as they pined and died of anaemia, so we, unless we repent, must perish in a paroxysm of black-blood apoplexy. And this prospect becomes more certain, when you reflect that the physician as we know him is not, like other men and things, a being of gradual growth, of slow evolution: from Adam to the middle of the last century the world saw nothing even in the least resembling him. No son of Paian *he*, but a fatherless, full-grown birth from the incessant matrix of Modern Time, so motherly of monstrous litters of "Gorgon and Hydra and Chimaeras dire"; you will understand what I mean when you consider the quite recent date of, say, the introduction of anaesthetics or antiseptics, the discovery of the knee-jerk, bacteriology, or even of such a doctrine as the circulation of the blood. We are at this very time, if I mistake not, on the verge of new insights which will enable man to laugh at disease—laugh at it in the sense of over-ruling its natural tendency to produce death, not by any means in the sense of destroying its ever-expanding *existence*. Do you know that at this moment your hospitals are crammed with beings in human likeness suffering from a thousand obscure and subtly-ineradicable ills, all of whom, if left alone, would die almost at once, but ninety in the hundred of whom will, as it is, be sent forth "cured," like missionaries of hell, and the horrent shapes of Night and Acheron, to mingle in the pure river of humanity the poison-taint of their protean vileness? Do you know that in your schools one-quarter of the children are already purblind? Have you gauged the importance of your tremendous consumption of quack catholicons, of the fortunes derived from their sale, of the spread of modern nervous disorders, of toothless youth and thrice loathsome age among the helot-classes? Do you know that in the course of my late journey to London, I walked from Piccadilly Circus to Hyde Park Corner, during which time I observed some five hundred people, of whom twenty-seven only were perfectly healthy, well-formed men, and eighteen healthy, beautiful women? On every hand—with a thrill of intensest joy, I say it!—is to be seen, if not yet commencing civilisation, then progress, progress— wide as the world—toward it: only here—at the heart—is there decadence, fatty degeneration. Brain-evolution—and favouring airs—and the ripening time—and the silent Will of God, of God—all these in conspiracy seem to be behind, urging the whole ship's company of us to some undreamable luxury of glory—when lo, this check, artificial, evitable. Less death, more disease—that is the sad, the unnatural record; children especially—so sensitive to the physician's art—living on by hundreds of thousands, bearing within them the germs of wide-spreading sorrow, who in former times would have died. And if you consider that the proper function of the doctor is the strictly limited one of curing the curable, rather than of self-gloriously perpetuating the incurable, you may find it difficult to give a quite rational answer to this simple question: *why?* Nothing is so sure as that to the unit it is a cruelty; nothing so certain as that to humanity it is a wrong; to say that such and such an one was sent by the All Wise, and must *therefore* be not merely permitted, but elaborately coaxed and forced, to live, is to utter a blasphemy against Man at which even the ribald tongue of a priest might falter; and as a matter of fact, society, in just contempt for this species of argument, never hesitates to hang, for its own imagined good, its heaven-sent catholics, protestants, sheep, sheep-stealers, etc. What then, you ask, would I do with these unholy ones? To save the State would I pierce them with a sword, or leave them to the slow throes of their agonies? Ah, do not expect me to answer that question—I do not know what to answer. The whole spirit of the present is one of a broad and beautiful, if quite thoughtless, humanism, and I, a child of the present, cannot but be borne along by it, coerced into sympathy with it. "Beautiful" I say: for if anywhere in the world you have seen a sight more beautiful than a group of hospital *savants* bending with endless scrupulousness over a little pauper child, concentering upon its frailty the whole human skill and wisdom of ages, so have not I. Here have you the full realisation of a parable diviner than that of the man who went down from Jerusalem to Jericho. Beautiful then; with at least surface beauty, like the serpent *lachesis mutus*; but, like many beautiful things, deadly too, *in*human. And, on the whole, an answer will have to be found. As for me, it is a doubt which has often agitated me, whether the central dogma of Judaism and Christianity alike can, after all, be really one of the inner verities of this our earthly being—the dogma, that by the shedding of the innocent blood, and by that alone, shall the race of man find cleansing and salvation. Will no agony of reluctance overcome the necessity that one man die, "so that the whole people perish not"? Can it be true that by nothing less than the "three days of pestilence" shall the land be purged of its stain, and is this old divine alternative about to confront us in new, modern form? Does the inscrutable Artemis indeed demand offerings of human blood to suage her anger? Most sad that man should ever need, should ever have needed, to foul his hand in the [Greek: musaron aima] of his own veins! But what is, is. And can it be fated that the most advanced civilisation of the future shall needs have in it, as the first and chief element of its glory, the most barbarous of all the rituals of barbarism—the immolation of hecatombs which wail a muling human wail? Is it indeed part of man's strange destiny through the deeps of Time that he one day bow his back to the duty of pruning himself as a garden, so that he run not to a waste wilderness? Shall the physician, the *accoucheur*, of the time to come be expected, and commanded, to do on the ephod and breast-plate, anoint his head with the oil of gladness, and add to the function of healer the function of Sacrificial Priest? These you say, are wild, dark questions. Wild enough, dark enough. We know how Sparta—the "man-taming Sparta" Simonides calls her—answered them. Here was the complete subordination of all unit-life to the well-being of the Whole. The child, immediately on his entry into the world, fell under the control of the State: it was not left to the judgment of his parents, as elsewhere, whether he should be brought up or not, but a commission of the Phyle in which he was born decided the question. If he was weakly, if he had any bodily unsightliness, he was exposed on a place called Taygetus, and so perished. It was a consequence of this that never did the sun in his course light on man half so godly stalwart, on woman half so houri-lovely, as in stern and stout old Sparta. Death, like all mortal, they must bear; disease, once and for all, they were resolved to have done with. The word which they used to express the idea "ugly," meant also "hateful," "vile," "disgraceful" —and I need hardly point out to you the significance of that fact alone; for they considered—and rightly—that there is no sort of natural reason why every denizen of earth should not be perfectly hale, integral, sane, beautiful—if only very moderate pains be taken to procure this divine result. One fellow, indeed, called Nancleidas, grew a little too fat to please the sensitive eyes of the Spartans: I believe he was periodically whipped. Under a system so very barbarous, the super-sweet, egoistic voice of the club-footed poet Byron would, of course, never have been heard: one brief egoistic "lament" on Taygetus, and so an end. It is not, however, certain that the world could not have managed very well without Lord Byron. The one thing that admits of no contradiction is that it cannot manage without the holy citizen, and that disease, to men and to nations, can have but one meaning, annihilation near or ultimate. At any rate, from these remarks, you will now very likely be able to arrive at some understanding of the wording of the advertisements which I sent to the papers.'

Zaleski, having delivered himself of this singular *tirade*, paused: replaced the sepulchral relief in its niche: drew a drapery of silver cloth over his bare feet and the hem of his antique garment of Babylon: and then continued:

'After some time the answer to the advertisement at length arrived; but what was my disgust to find that it was perfectly unintelligible to me. I had asked for a date and an address: the reply came giving a date, and an address, too—but an address wrapped up in cypher, which, of course, I, as a supposed member of the society, was expected to be able to read. At any rate, I now knew the significance of the incongruous circumstance that the Latin proverb *mens sana etc.* should be adopted as the motto of a Greek society; the significance lay in this, that the motto *contained an address*—the address of their meeting-place, or at least, of their chief meeting-place. I was now confronted with the task of solving—and of solving quickly, without the loss of an hour—this enigma; and I confess that it was only by the most violent and extraordinary concentration of what I may call the dissecting faculty, that I was able to do so in good time. And yet there was no special difficulty in the matter. For looking at the motto as it stood in cypher, the first thing I perceived was that, in order to read the secret, the heart-shaped figure must be left out of consideration, if there was any *consistency* in the system of cyphers at all, for it belonged to a class of symbols quite distinct from that of all the others, not being, like them, a picture-letter. Omitting this, therefore, and taking all the other vowels and consonants whether actually represented in the device or not, I now got the proverb in the form *mens sana in ... pore sano*. I wrote this down, and what instantly struck me was the immense, the altogether unusual, number of *liquids* in the motto—six in all, amounting to no less than one-third of the total number of letters! Putting these all together you get *mnnnnr*, and you can see that the very appearance of the "m's" and "n's" (especially when *written*) running into one another, of itself suggests a stream of water. Having previously arrived at the conclusion of London as the meeting-place, I could not now fail to go on to the inference of *the Thames*; there, or near there, would I find those whom I sought. The letters "mnnnnr," then, meant the Thames: what did the still remaining letters mean? I now took these remaining letters, placing them side by side: I got aaa, sss, ee, oo, p and i. Juxtaposing these nearly in the order indicated by the frequency of their occurrence, and their place in the Roman alphabet, you at once and inevitably get the word *Aesopi*. And now I was fairly startled by this symmetrical proof of the exactness of my own deductions in other respects, but, above all, far above all, by the occurrence of that word "*Aesopi*." For who was Aesopus? He was a slave who was freed for his wise and witful sallies: he is therefore typical of the liberty of the wise—their moral manumission from temporary and narrow law; he was also a close friend of Croesus: he is typical, then, of the union of wisdom with wealth—true wisdom with real wealth; lastly, and above all, he was thrown by the Delphians from a rock on account of his wit: he is typical, therefore, of death—the shedding of blood—as a result of wisdom, this thought being an elaboration of Solomon's great maxim, "in much wisdom is much sorrow." But how accurately all this fitted in with what would naturally be the doctrines of the men on whose track I was! I could no longer doubt the justness of my reasonings, and immediately, while you slept, I set off for London.

'Of my haps in London I need not give you a very particular account. The meeting was to be held on the 15th, and by the morning of the 13th I had reached a place called Wargrave, on the Thames. There I hired a light canoe, and thence proceeded down the river in a somewhat zig-zag manner, narrowly examining the banks on either side, and keeping a sharp out-look for some board, or sign, or house, that would seem to betoken any sort of connection with the word "Aesopi." In this way I passed a fruitless day, and having reached the shipping region, made fast my craft, and in a spirit of *diablerie* spent the night in a common lodging-house, in the company of the most remarkable human beings, characterised by an odour of alcohol, and a certain obtrusive *bonne camaraderie* which the prevailing fear of death could not altogether repress. By dawn of the 14th I was on my journey again—on, and ever on. Eagerly I longed for a sight of the word I sought: but I had misjudged the men against whose cunning I had measured my own. I should have remembered more consistently that they were no ordinary men. As I was destined to find, there lay a deeper, more cabalistic meaning in the motto than any I had been able to dream of. I had proceeded on my pilgrimage down the river a long way past Greenwich, and had now reached a desolate and level reach of land stretching away on either hand. Paddling my boat from the right to the left bank, I came to a spot where a little arm of the river ran up some few yards into the land. The place wore a specially dreary and deserted aspect: the land was flat, and covered with low shrubs. I rowed into this arm of shallow water and rested on my oar, wearily bethinking myself what was next to be done. Looking round, however, I saw to my surprise that at the end of this arm there was a short narrow pathway—a winding road—leading from the river-bank. I stood up in the boat and followed its course with my eyes. It was met by another road also winding among the bushes, but in a slightly different direction. At the end of this was a little, low, high-roofed, round house, without doors or windows. And then—and then—tingling now with a thousand raptures—I beheld a pool of water near this structure, and then another low house, a counterpart of the first—and then, still leading on in the same direction, another pool—and then a great rock, heart-shaped—and then another winding road—and then another pool of water. All was a model—*exact to the minutest particular*—of the device on the papyrus! The first long-waved line was the river itself; the three short-waved lines were the arm of the river and the two pools; the three snakes were the three winding roads; the two triangles representing the letter #A# were the two high-roofed round houses; the heart was the rock! I sprang, now thoroughly excited, from the boat, and ran in headlong haste to the end of the last lake. Here there was a rather thick and high growth of bushes, but peering among them, my eye at once caught a white oblong board supported on a stake: on this, in black letters, was marked the words, "DESCENSUS AESOPI." It was necessary, therefore, to go *down*: the meeting-place was subterranean. It was without difficulty that I discovered a small opening in the ground, half hidden by the underwood; from the orifice I found that a series of wooden steps led directly downwards, and I at once boldly descended. No sooner, however, had I touched the bottom than I was confronted by an ancient man in Hellenic apparel, armed with the Greek *ziphos* and *peltè*. His eyes, accustomed to the gloom, pierced me long with an earnest scrutiny.

"'You are a Spartan?" he asked at length.

"'Yes," I answered promptly.

"'Then how is it you do not know that I am stone deaf?"

'I shrugged, indicating that for the moment I had forgotten the fact.

'"You *are* a Spartan?" he repeated.

'I nodded with emphasis.

'"Then, how is it you omit to make the sign?"

'Now, you must not suppose that at this point I was nonplussed, for in that case you would not give due weight to the strange inherent power of the mind to rise to the occasion of a sudden emergency—to stretch itself long to the length of an event; I do not hesitate to say that *no* combination of circumstances can defeat a vigorous brain fully alert, and in possession of itself. With a quickness to which the lightning-flash is tardy, I remembered that this was a spot indicated by the symbols on the papyrus: I remembered that this same papyrus was always placed under the *tongue* of the dead; I remembered, too, that among that very nation whose language had afforded the motto, to "turn up the *thumb*" (*pollicem vertere*) was a symbol significant of death. I touched the under surface of my tongue with the tip of my thumb. The aged man was appeased. I passed on, and examined the place.

'It was simply a vast circular hall, the arched roof of which was supported on colonnades of what I took to be pillars of porphyry. Down the middle and round the sides ran tables of the same material; the walls were clothed in hangings of sable velvet, on which, in infinite reproduction, was embroidered in cypher the motto of the society. The chairs were cushioned in the same stuff. Near the centre of the circle stood a huge statue, of what really seemed to me to be pure beaten gold. On the great ebon base was inscribed the word [Greek: LUKURGOS]. From the roof swung by brazen chains a single misty lamp.

'Having seen this much I reascended to the land of light, and being fully resolved on attending the meeting on the next day or night, and not knowing what my fate might then be, I wrote to inform you of the means by which my body might be traced. 'But on the next day a new thought occurred to me: I reasoned thus: "these men are not common assassins; they wage a too rash warfare against diseased life, but not against life in general. In all probability they have a quite immoderate, quite morbid reverence for the sanctity of healthy life. They will not therefore take mine, *unless* they suppose me to be the only living outsider who has a knowledge of their secret, and therefore think it absolutely necessary for the carrying out of their beneficent designs that my life should be sacrificed. I will therefore prevent such a motive from occurring to them by communicating to another their whole secret, and—if the necessity should arise—*letting them know* that I have done so, without telling them who that other is. Thus my life will be assured." I therefore wrote to you on that day a full account of all I had discovered, giving you to understand, however, on the envelope, that you need not examine the contents for some little time.

'I waited in the subterranean vault during the greater part of the next day; but not till midnight did the confederates gather. What happened at that meeting I shall not disclose, even to you. All was sacred—solemn—full of awe. Of the choral hymns there sung, the hierophantic ritual, liturgies, paeans, the gorgeous symbolisms—of the wealth there represented, the culture, art, self-sacrifice—of the mingling of all the tongues of Europe—I shall not speak; nor shall I repeat names which you would at once recognise as familiar to you—though I may, perhaps, mention that the "Morris," whose name appears on the papyrus sent to me is a well-known *littérateur* of that name. But this in confidence, for some years at least.

'Let me, however, hurry to a conclusion. My turn came to speak. I rose undaunted, and calmly disclosed myself; during the moment of hush, of wide-eyed paralysis that ensued, I declared that fully as I coincided with their views in general, I found myself unable to regard their methods with approval—these I could not but consider too rash, too harsh, too premature. My voice was suddenly drowned by one universal, earth-shaking roar of rage and contempt, during which I was surrounded on all sides, seized, pinioned, and dashed on the central table. All this time, in the hope and love of life, I passionately shouted that I was not the only living being who shared in their secret. But my voice was drowned, and drowned again, in the whirling tumult. None heard me. A powerful and little-known anaesthetic—the means by which all their murders have been accomplished—was now produced. A cloth, saturated with the fluid, was placed on my mouth and nostrils. I was stifled. Sense failed. The incubus of the universe blackened down upon my brain. How I tugged at the mandrakes of speech! was a locked pugilist with language! In the depth of my extremity the half-thought, I remember, floated, like a mist, through my fading consciousness, that now perhaps—now—there was silence around me; that *now*, could my palsied lips find dialect, I should be heard, and understood. My whole soul rose focussed to the effort—my body jerked itself upwards. At that moment I knew my spirit truly great, genuinely sublime. For I *did* utter something—my dead and shuddering tongue *did* babble forth some coherency. Then I fell back, and all was once more the ancient Dark. On the next day when I woke, I was lying on my back in my little boat, placed there by God knows whose hands. At all events, one thing was clear—I *had* uttered something—I was saved. With what of strength remained to me I reached the place where I had left your *calèche*, and started on my homeward way. The necessity to sleep was strong upon me, for the fumes of the anaesthetic still clung about my brain; hence, after my long journey, I fainted on my passage through the house, and in this condition you found me.

'Such then is the history of my thinkings and doings in connection with this ill-advised confraternity: and now that their cabala is known to others—to how many others *they* cannot guess—I think it is not unlikely that we shall hear little more of the Society of Sparta.'

THE END

Milton Keynes UK
Ingram Content Group UK Ltd.
UKHW030720041024
449263UK00004B/356